SYNTAX OF THE RIVER

The Pattern Which Connects

BARRY LOPEZ

in conversation with
JULIA MARTIN

TERRA FIRMA BOOKS /
TRINITY UNIVERSITY PRESS
SAN ANTONIO, TEXAS

Terra Firma Books, an imprint of
Trinity University Press
San Antonio, Texas 78212

Cover design by Rebecca Lown

Book design by Amnet

Cover photo by Tim Giraudier (beautifuloregon.com), used courtesy of McKenzie
River Trust

Author photo, Julia Martin and Barry Lopez, 2018, by Debra Gwartney

ISBN 978-1-59534-989-7 paper
ISBN 978-1-59534-990-3 ebook

CIP data on file at the Library of Congress

26   25   24   23   22 | 5   4   3   2   1

For Debra
and for the McKenzie River

The river is not a thing. [. . .] It is an expression of biological life in dynamic relation to everything around it—the salmon within, the violet-green swallow swooping its surface, alder twigs floating its current, a mountain lion sipping its bank water, the configurations of basalt that break its flow and give it timbre and tone.

— Barry Lopez, "The Naturalist"

CONTENTS

THE SOUND
OF WATER

JULIA MARTIN

There was a little black plastic bear on the dashboard of the truck when Barry Lopez fetched me from the airport. I noticed because it was just like the one I'd been carrying in my backpack since arriving in the United States. "The polar bear's elsewhere in the truck," he said, "the big mother."

Bears in the old Toyota truck seemed about right. For decades Barry had pondered the conundrum of human people's relation to other beings, traveling across the world to explore the mystery, and returning to write luminous prose that somehow combined lyrical observation with a great deal of information. His writing spoke directly to work in literature and ecology that I'd been doing in South Africa for some years. And after we met through our mutual friend Gary Snyder, Barry became a dear friend too, even a teacher.

So in fall 2010, I visited him at his home in Finn Rock, Oregon. The formal part of the visit involved recording a conversation about his work that extended over three days. For this, we sat at the window of a small wood cabin at the edge of the McKenzie River, with my little black bear on the table beside us. During the rest of the time we drove for hours through deep green forests, slowing the truck to a walk so as to get out and look at Douglas fir cones with the little mouse tails peeping out, a piece of horsetail snapped off and used for cleaning teeth, wild garlic chewed, mushrooms in the damp near a waterfall, a Townsend's chipmunk, a chickadee, a marten crossing our path. And we told many stories: stories of bear and elk and mountain lion passing through, stories of home and away, and stories of the interwoven joys and sadnesses of our lives. In all this, Barry's capacity for openness, focus, and seriousness were unrelenting. It was an intense time, and I felt at once exhausted and elevated, the recipient of something irreplaceable. Three words in my journal noted what seemed like the heart of it: respect, kindness, suffering.

On returning to Cape Town, I had the recording transcribed. The typist noted that the sound of water was continuous in the background throughout the interview and said working on it had been a gift of peace at the end of the year. This was good to hear, and I sent the text to Barry to edit, hoping to publish it soon. But there it sat. He kept meaning to work on the conversation, but it was really long, and rather more rambling in structure than he'd have preferred. And of course other things kept intervening. His massive book project, *Horizon*, which was finally completed in 2018, took up most of his writing energy. Then there was a serious cancer diagnosis, and the years of diminishing strength and determined courage that followed. Curiously, the deferred publication of the interview became a background thread to our contact over the years, a conversation in itself. Barry would feel remorseful that he hadn't done it, and I would remind him that the main thing was the opportunity the visit had given us to be together.

Two years now since his death on Christmas Day of 2020, the deep blue agapanthus I planted for him are flowering again, and it feels at last time to share our conversation. His wife, Debra Gwartney, whom I met on a later visit and who became a dear friend, is keen for others to read it. And I think Barry would have been too. His words from a letter in 2015 are a poignant nudge to complete the project. "I've no intention of letting that interview slide," he wrote. "We worked hard on it and I'm determined to do my part with it. It is a beautiful record of our time together, yes, but there is something else there more than worthy of our continued attention. The ball is in my court and one day I will surprise you by returning your serve."

CONVER**SATIONS**

PATTERN

The quality of Barry's attention was extraordinary. He had the capacity to speak thoughtfully and at great length without a pause, his gaze held in earnest focus. And he could just as well remain quite still and silent for long spaces: listening, seeing, touching, breathing. In all this, he lived anchored in the being of one particular place. For all the journeys of intrepid exploration and adventure across the planet that we know from his writing, it was to this place that he always returned: the thirty-eight acres of deep forest and the reach of the McKenzie River below the house where he lived for fifty years. This negotiation between silence and speech, seclusion and engagement, made for a very fine and highly informed capacity for awareness as well as a powerful desire to communicate it. For while his inclinations were profoundly contemplative, there was also a strong sense of urgency to speak, to share the vision, to write, to help.

On the first day of our conversation, he begins by contemplating awareness itself. Reflecting on a lifetime of watching the river, he describes something of the quality of attention he has learned from intimacy with the place itself: a finely tuned sense of the distinction between silence and stillness, of the rich complexities of the present moment, of the syntax of myriad things in their lively interrelationships. In all there's a perception of the river as a living animal and of the pattern which connects. The stream of thought then meanders from stories about the miracle of Chinook salmon who return on the same day each year to the same place in the river, into the terrifying craziness of a human society focused on "me" and "mine," the suicidal impact of the profit motive, and on to the wonders of the Prado, the Louvre, a glorious symphony.

It was late afternoon, and we were sitting at the window of a timber cabin at the edge of the water. Whenever anyone came by—six female mergansers flying upriver into the sun, a great blue heron hunting—Barry would follow the thread of their presence for as long as it took, and he'd tell their stories.

This meant that whatever he might be saying about the terrors of the global environmental crisis, or the insanity of US politics, or the challenges of taking a position of resistance as a writer, or even the crucial need for reconciliation and compassion . . . it was continually being interrupted by whatever was actually going on in the lively ecosystem of the river. The effect of this was not digression but a conscious resituating of the present-tense urgencies of our human dialogue in the deep continuities of the nonhuman. Whatever our words might be attempting to say, this form of conversation kept bringing us back to an ongoing nonverbal conversation with the immediacy of everything else.

This experience of being a finely attentive participant in the community of all beings is perhaps Barry's core teaching. Over decades he developed a practice of awareness that was endlessly curious and enthralled by the living world, what he calls here its pattern or syntax. This meant too that he was consequently terrified by the portents of its destruction. As a writer his task, then, was to put this combination of wonder and terror to work. As he said that afternoon, expressing an attitude that became more explicit in recent years, "I write in order to help."

JM

JULIA MARTIN: Barry, you've said this place is a teacher. What does it teach?

BARRY LOPEZ: When I moved here in 1970, I was very active as a landscape photographer as well as a writer. I was out probably every day photographing. And that meant the line and the color and the volumes of space were things that drew my attention all the time. I guess the aesthetic question was, How are these related? And how are these related in time? Now, by watching the river and the trees over forty years, I can look at the river from the house and tell whether it's raining or what the season is. The water has a slightly different color during the four seasons, depending on how much snow and glacial melt is in it. And the parts of the river that are not visible in the summer are visible in the winter, because of the loss of leaves of deciduous trees.

One thing I did for a while would be to pick out a certain rock, like that one down there, and photograph it at two-thousandths of a second. That would give me an image that is not apparent to my eye but which for another eye, able to absorb information discretely in much shorter units of time, would be apparent. And then I would come back during a full moon and photograph from exactly the same position on a bank. In a twenty-minute time exposure, the film would fail. I would have reciprocity failure, meaning that the colors were false—the film would fail to register colors in approximately the way we see them. But it would also eliminate all the random—or what we would call random—movement in the water, and you would see something not usually apparent to you. That would be what a chaos philosopher might call a deeper attractor, or an organizing principle underneath what seemed to be chaotic. It showed you there *was* a here. It was just impossible for you to pick up.

That was one of the ways I came to understand the river as a kind of animal. It is a convenience of Western culture that we divide the world into plants and animals and minerals. But . . . just to pick somebody, a British explorer named Ralph Bagnold wrote a book in the 1930s called *Libyan Sands* about his experiences in the Libyan desert. He had become very interested in sand dunes, and he monitored them. At one place he watched two sand dunes converge and separate and continue on their paths. But they left a small sand dune in their wake. So, he asks a question in that book which prompted the question for me. He says, "Was I watching a biological or a geological phenomenon?"

Part of what distinguishes the river from other animals is that its entire life history, its ontogeny if you will, is apparent in the moment. We could walk twenty miles up the river to the source of the river, or twenty miles, thirty miles, down the river, and we would see its beginning and its end. All of its life is available in the moment, except those parts of its life that are seasonally specific. If you watch the water—you're here now in the fall—you will see that there are leaves floating on the water that are falling out of the alders and the ashes and the maples. But there are also leaves that are sodden; they are riding in the river below the surface, and the water is clear so you can see them. When you compare the speeds with which they are moving, it tells you that the water on the surface of the river is moving more slowly than the water just below the surface because there is no coefficient of friction from the air. And if you *really* study the water, then you will see that on the bottom there are leaves just sitting there. This is why small animals can wander around on the bottom of rivers that are moving very swiftly because the water at the bottom is moving in a series of back eddies that create a lot of still water at the very bottom.

The more you watch the river, the more you understand what it means to apply the adjective "alive." And it's in those ways, just with regard to the river, the birds, or other components of the place that we separate out and name, that you begin to get an understanding of what . . . of what this place is. I think for any writer, the place itself is not all that important. It's your *intimacy* with the place that's really important. You can learn about God anywhere is what it comes down to. You just have to pay attention.

Many years ago in Alaska—I think it was in a village called Savoonga on Saint Lawrence Island in the northern Bering Sea—I was talking with a Yupik Eskimo man about his ability to hunt in the pack ice, in the moving ice. I asked him whether he'd get disoriented when a big floe of ice was rotating. You see, there is no flux to the light there. You can't tell by looking at the sky where the sun is because there is no sense of rays of light coming from one direction instead of another. So, it's very easy not to know north from south because it all looks the same, the ice and the overcast sky. And he said, "Well, you know, it's just now"—he might have been in his fifties—"it's just *now* that I think I begin to understand the ice." And he'd been living there all his life. Then he said, "And now I'm really too old to hunt."

And I held on to that remark, not knowing why. But I know what he meant, now. I've been here for forty years, and I think I know . . . a little bit about the surface. I've wished I could speak with people who were older than me. And that I had the opportunity to speak with people who are younger than me, so that what this place gave to this animal, this human being, wouldn't be lost.

But the thing I would underscore, I guess, is that . . . you know, I'm not a naturalist, but I'm intensely interested in, and I would go so far as to say *enthralled* with, all the forms of life that are around me. I'm elevated when I see them animated. I'm elevated when I'm standing in the woods and I can understand the difference between silence and stillness, for example. Sometimes it's still but it's not quiet. And sometimes it's silent but it's not still.

When you parse the experience like that, it trains you to approach ideas in the same way. What I would like to underscore is that being intimate with a place helps you understand the pathways to become intimate with complex ideas.

You know, I've got to think that the story, storytelling, came about in part because it served the desire that people had to clarify what it is that they were feeling or imagining. And they would, I have to think, make reference to something outside the self, as an equivalent to what they were feeling. They would pause and look, sweep a hand across the play of light in a tree that was upwelling in a storm, and say, "Well, I . . . *that's* how I feel now." In that way, people understood that there is a connection here that is not biological, or not solely biological.

I guess that's what I've been doing for forty years: trying to go to cities and look at art, talk to people in other cultures, and apprentice myself to people who can teach me how to do simple things their way. And then coming back here and just walking around in the woods, trying to sort it out and see the emergence of a pattern. I think when you're young you want to learn the names of everything. This is a beaver, this is spring Chinook, this is a rainbow trout, this is osprey, elk over there. But it's the *syntax* that you really are after. Anybody can develop the vocabulary. It's the relationships that are important. And it's the discerning of this three-dimensional set of relationships that awakens you to how complex this is at any one moment.

Then, of course, the next thought is that there is not one moment. Five minutes ago the river was different from what it is now. If we were acutely aware, we would know that because the sonic landscape changes.

When I'm down at the river, I can tell stages of the river just by listening. Its voice is completely different when there's two or three inches more, or two or three inches less water there, because it moves over the rocks in a different way. And what some would, I guess, call cacophony—and maybe it is—to somebody with a more sophisticated ear than I, it's not cacophony. It's, you know, maybe a version of arhythmic, atonal music. John Cage could sit here and say, "Oh, yeah, well," and see some deep organizing principle in the sound of the water, the way you could see, by shooting it in moonlight for twenty minutes, you could see the deep resolution of the laminar flow of water. Then it hits one of those rocks. And then it breaks up and goes around it. Heisenberg was famously asked, "If you get to heaven, what would you ask God?" And he said, "Well, I would ask him about relativity and about turbulence. I'd expect him to have an answer about the first." Meaning that turbulence, or chaos, is more complex, it's more difficult to wrap your mind around chaos than it is to wrap it around relativity. And this is the orchestra of chaos right here in front of us. And it's *so* interesting to me always, that the world of commerce and vacations and going to town is, you know, fifty feet away.

Salmon came in here, this month. Chinook salmon.

They come across the Columbia River bar in February, which is the beginning of our spring, and they come up the Columbia River and up the Willamette River, and they make the turn into the McKenzie River here. And they seem to come in two pulses. They come up in May and June and hang out in some of these big, deep holes, twenty, thirty feet deep. They just hang out there for a couple of months. And then another pulse comes upriver in late August and early September, and they move right onto the gravel bars, right away, and the females start building their nests. Then they spawn and die.

I've noticed some time ago that they come like the swallows famous to Americans, the swallows of Capistrano. They come on the same day. So, if you measured twenty-four hours either side of noon on September 17, the salmon would be here. It's been like that for forty years. And I become anxious, you know, on the evening of the seventeenth if they aren't here. I've gone down in darkness, in total darkness, on the seventeenth. I've done it so often, I don't really need to see. I just come down through the woods and navigate aurally, navigate by the sound. And when I'm standing next to the river, even though it's like this, I can sort out the sound of a caudal fin moving in the water. And I know they are there. I can hear that they're there. Then in the morning I'll come down and I'll *see* that they're there. So, that awareness, I guess, that the landscape is open to us in ways that we wouldn't immediately think of . . . I think that is an important part of the way we experience the world.

When you go to another country and you're dealing with a language you don't speak, and with customs around the consumption of food that you're not familiar with, and hours for sleeping and being awake, you can find some other way than your accustomed way. And that kind of experience leads you to what I think is one of the most important parts of international politics now. That is the awareness of, and the accommodation of oneself to, the existence of profoundly different epistemologies that should not be changed. If you want everybody to have the same truth, or to believe in the same things, then you're talking about the loss of tension and the collapse of the world.

Our trouble seems to be that, you know, our primate heritage, which is apparent in watching the behavior of chimpanzees and bonobos, is that we're keenly interested in ourselves and opposed to others. That's deep in our tissues. And with the kind of world we've built, that's not going to work. So, those human beings who have the very strongest residue of the kind of patrolling behavior and violence that troops of chimpanzees have, those people would like the world to be, I think, arranged in a way that suits their habits and their desires. But a lot of people die that way. And we have created a chemical environment that is killing people left and right, quickly or slowly, through cancer, for example.

It just doesn't make sense anymore to have these ideas about "me" and "mine" and the terrible burden that has been created by so-called advanced nations about the primacy of ownership, the ownership of food. Or, you know, the terrifying thing in the United States, this idea that nothing is exempt from the application of a kind of economics that's meant for profit. I mean, how can you make the care of another, the professional care of another person's body, be informed by a profit motive? Even a fifth grade kid can see there is something that doesn't really add up here.

So, for me as a writer, I live here and I'm informed by this place. And the way it informs me helps me understand a lot of the things my species does that are suicidal. It's not up to me to say that they are suicidal, but I would feel like a traitor to my teachers here if I never said a thing, never mentioned it.

MARTIN: Part of what they are teaching seems to be an active awareness, a quality of attention. And with it comes stillness and silence, a kind of practice. You are required by this context to be quite still and quite silent.

LOPEZ: Yes.

MARTIN: That often comes through in the writing: a sense of presence and awareness and attention. Do you think that practice of attention is a kind of act of resistance?

LOPEZ: Oh yeah, I do. I mean, I do have a television and I watch it. But about the only thing I watch are sports, or we have some of these serial dramas in the States that are really well written and well acted, and I'll watch those once in a while. But for the most part, music is not on in the house, the television is not on. *Nothing* much is on. And I'm very comfortable with that. I don't have email and, you know, the phone rings once in a while and the world uses forms of communication that I don't participate in. That is good for me, because there are fewer letters and fewer phone calls from people who'd rather email or not communicate with you at all.

That's not to say that my assistant doesn't intervene here and take care of a lot of that kind of stuff. But . . .

I sometimes think of myself as a sort of control group. There's very little distraction around me. I'm not running from one place to another, answering the phone, and multi-tasking. I don't have anything to multitask. Oh, I do, you know, when I clean the kitchen and do the laundry and do all of that at once, and get it all done, but I spend a lot of time not doing much of anything except participating in what's going on around me.

Just standing out there, watching the wind. Standing at the windows of the house, watching light break up in the trees. Or coming down at night and opening the front door and standing on the porch and just listening, listening for what's going on in the dark. And leaving the windows open in the bedroom so I can hear what's going on at night. I guess I would become afraid if I weren't anchored in a place where I feel . . . I feel I'm always learning a more refined way of looking, listening, and touching.

And when my grandson is with me, I try to ensure that he's picking things up and tasting some things—not everything—and feeling things, palpating things and putting things together. I would show him, "If we see this plant, then we have a good chance of seeing this other plant. Let's see if we can find it." And you know, he'll find it and he'll understand that there is a familial relationship there with those plants. And when he goes to school, he won't always be thinking of one idea separate from another idea. He'll say, "If we are going to be talking about this, then this must be part of the conversation." That's what I want to stimulate with him.

I grew up in an agricultural part of Southern California, and my focus was on trees and animals and the wind. And then my mother remarried and we moved to New York City. It was *just* the right age for me, eleven years old, and I put all of that energy into something completely different, which was to go to museums and to go to the theater and participate in the cultural life of New York. When I went to Europe when I was seventeen, I was eager to see all these things that I knew would be in the Prado, or in the Louvre, or at the National Gallery. I wanted to see those things, I wanted to be present to them, and I saw them as a part of my culture that I cherish. And I still do. But I don't separate that childhood experience with the river, the trees, the wind from the world that I see in paintings, or the way I hear a symphony played and imagine the four parts of the symphony connected, and how revealing one is of the other. You know, there are parts of symphonies that, to my ear, are a commentary on what came earlier, in the same way that in a novel you develop something that comes back and picks up the stitch that was dropped in the first chapter and pulls it forward. So, the similarity in the patterns of creation for a novel—or for some poems and pieces of formal music—it's all embedded right here.

The difference is, I guess, that the river is never going to tell you that you're wrong. But in school, someone will tell you that you have the wrong interpretation of a novel. So, when you're out in the landscape like this, you can examine the shape of your own prejudices without fear of reprisal. The tree is not going to strike you down for getting it wrong. The tree is indifferent to your way of knowing. It's part of a world that you stepped away from for cultural reasons, and it's not going to come and rescue you, or it doesn't have really an interest in you and your fate [*laughter*].

But when you participate with everything around you, it goes a long way toward undermining what is I guess called existential loneliness. You can't walk in these landscapes and really be an existentialist. There are too many invitations to be a participant in the world.

MARTIN: So, with a little boy like your grandson, or with a reader even, you are talking about a kind of education of the imagination that could go wherever it wants to go.

LOPEZ: Absolutely.

MARTIN: It's not about nature as some sort of—

LOPEZ: No, no, no—

MARTIN: —separate category. Rocks and plants and trees.

LOPEZ: No.

MARTIN: You started off in Southern California, which was very rural, and then you moved to New York. And by then you had a kind of developed awareness that was able to adjust and respond to a city.

LOPEZ: Yeah. You know, the first time I saw a Vermeer, in the Frick Collection in New York, I could say, "Wow. He was paying attention to the light." And it's just that simple.

MARTIN: And the dominant culture is working in the opposite direction of that sort of awareness? Is that what you're implying?

LOPEZ: The dominant culture to me seems pathologically bent on distraction. It seems more driven by *fear* than love of anything. But, you know, in fairness to people, the world we made is extremely challenging. You can be a virtuoso at that keyboard in front of a computer terminal, but the idea that you're in control is ridiculous. And the idea that this is a complexity greater than the complexity just outside this window is naïve. If you're inclined to seek a position of authority or power, and you begin to ignore these things, you know, you're going to founder. And to me at the moment, American culture is foundering. Its system of governance has been taken over by people whose motivations really have to do with the enforcement of one epistemology over another. And—

Female mergansers! Can you see them? There are six of them, just above the water there, just flying along about fifty miles an hour. . . . They're gone now. They were just caught then in the light.

MARTIN: Wow.

LOPEZ: All females. With something like that, you know, the first thing that comes into my mind is, Where are the men? And why aren't they here? And why are those women traveling together? And why do they *love* to be about eighteen inches off the water? They aren't going to be two feet off the water. They're not going to be forty feet off the water. So, it just starts a pattern of seeing them, and they are way better at being them than anybody else, you know. They have their own way of doing things. And why would they be flying downriver this late in the afternoon? Right into that sun?

MARTIN: Going home?

LOPEZ: I saw a female merganser here one day with twenty-one ducklings—

MARTIN: Twenty-one!

LOPEZ: Yeah, they adopt the ducklings of females that fall by the wayside for one reason or another. The thing I couldn't understand about her is that she was moving them across the river, and she would get them all up on a rock. And then at a certain moment, she'd push them and get them all to jump in the water. And then they'd race like hell to the next rock and get up on the rock. And I thought, *Well, why doesn't she just swim across the river with them?* It took me a while to figure out that when they're on a rock, they're not vulnerable to an osprey, those ducklings.

MARTIN: Okay.

LOPEZ: But when they're in the water they are. She knew that and she knew, Get 'em to a rock, get 'em to the next rock, get 'em to the next rock until we can get under these overhanging trees over here, and then we're going to be okay and we'll be in the water. The angle of attack for an osprey is gone. So, you know, when you start to study things like that, and say, "Well, I wonder why?" then that's how you understand something of the way in which the world is hinged.

But anyway, to return to the grim present, I think there has never been a time like this for paying attention to what's going on in the world that's not controlled by human beings. And all the social and economic schemes of organizing to a good end that we've done ourselves, or killed others for the refusal to do, are maybe not the best ideas at the moment. In a state of emergency, a democracy is not the best form of government to have. *Elders* is the best form of government to have. If the house is burning down, you don't have time to listen to 250 million people say what they think should be done. You have to put the fire out or there'll be no house.

People want to postpone the loss of their profits, for example. You know, there's a line—I may have overheard it in an airport or something—it was somebody who said, "But I don't want to lose my *stuff*!" Well, good luck! You're going to lose a *lot* of your stuff! And then you're going to say to yourself, "I wonder why I didn't make common cause with a group of people instead of common cause with just myself and what I wanted."

So, social upheaval is right around the corner. Environmental difficulties are going to get worse, not better. We can recycle all we want, and go green, and build wind farms and whatnot. But the change that's required has got to go really, really deep. And when you have hordes of religious fundamentalists in denial about global climate change, you shouldn't be angry. You should be terrified. Because, at least in the United States, the political power of that group of people is significant. They elected and reelected a president that involved the United States in a war in Iraq and Afghanistan, for no good reason.

But my political views are immaterial. They're there in that piece "Six Thousand Lessons." Really, who cares what I have to say? All I can do, and all I want to do, is write a story. And I hope the story stimulates a conversation.

That a nonfiction piece stimulates conversation. And that a short story, a piece of fiction, elevates a person to a point where they consider the things that are really important to them.

MARTIN: Yes.

LOPEZ: I want to make a *pattern* in a story that allows a person to say, "I remember what I forgot about what I meant my life to be. And I'm going to go do that now."

MARTIN: It sounds like what someone says about Mirara in "The Runner." That she makes you think about what you believe in when you're with her. It's a trope you come back to again and again in the short stories: a character who is usually quite a solitary person, or at least a person on their own, encountering somebody—or some being or situation—that offers some kind of teaching, and who brings them to a point of reassessing what their basis was.

LOPEZ: Right.

MARTIN: The story usually ends before any clear resolution. There's no kind of, "Ah, now I know what I'm going to do next."

LOPEZ: I think a good piece of fiction doesn't end on the page. That part of what you're trying to do is allow the pattern to come to full closure, in the mind of the individual reader, so that the story never gets to being didactic or having a point that you're trying to make. Nothing wrong with making a point in an essay, but I think there's something wrong with trying to make a point in a piece of fiction.

MARTIN: You know, when I read *Resistance* I felt quite ambivalent about that. I actually loved and shared the point of view that was coming through but tended to feel that the stories were just too clearly assembled to make that point. But maybe that's what the contemporary global crisis, the present emergency, demands? It's not that the stories are simply didactic. That would be putting it too strongly. But if I think of earlier collections, something like *Winter Count*, say, there is such integrity in terms of the presentation of image and person and narrative. Whereas with *Resistance*, I felt each time, yes, this is it, he's working out the issue of a person dealing with an old pain, and the possibility of healing and love.

LOPEZ: Well, I accept that. The stories in *Resistance* have much more to do with each other, of course, than in any other collection.

MARTIN: Yes, that's also part of it.

LOPEZ: And it was driven by . . . You know my friend Alan Magee who did those monoprints? I looked at those monoprints—I think that they were his reaction initially to the first Gulf War—and I was so taken with them. Alan had sent me smaller versions of them and I had them up around my workroom. And he and I would talk. We'd

wonder—because neither one of us is a political activist—
what was our ethical responsibility in a world like this.

MARTIN: It's the question, isn't it? Or a question.

LOPEZ: His response was to do the monoprints. He's my dear
friend, and I was moved by those images and I had them
around, and I knew I wanted to respond to them in some
way. And it turned out to be that *Resistance* was the way to
respond. You're certainly right that there's more of a *point*,
there's more of an urgency, I guess, in that collection.

MARTIN: Which I share, and I think it needs to be expressed.
But it raises for me questions about how a writer engages
in these times.

LOPEZ: Yeah. Well I think you just keep making your stories.
And realize that whatever skill you have, it's the skill of
making a story. It's not the skill of developing policy.

MARTIN: Right.

LOPEZ: That's for other people to do. But if you write good
stories, then people who are capable of writing good policy
will write better policy for having read the stories. Or at
least that's what seems to me. Maybe that's naïve, but it's
what I . . . what I believe. And you know, I write in order to
help. The way I help in the world is by writing. If I stand
up in front of an audience and am able to speak—great.
If I have something to say in a group setting with other
women and men—great. But the really important thing is

sitting in front of that typewriter. And that's what I want to do.

You know, I love to travel. And part of the reason that I travel is because the danger of being in a place like this is that, without intending to, you can get locked up in your own metaphor. So, if I go—

There are two female mergansers over there. See them? Very white breasts. One underneath the trees and right at the edge of the bank over there. I should have brought binoculars for you.

MARTIN: You really know what you are looking for!

LOPEZ: Yeah. They are very shy, so if we go out they might move. [*He gets up to go and see.*] But come on out. [*Both go and look at the mergansers on the river.*]

MARTIN: A historian friend said something to me recently about a book I'm writing that I've found quite strong. We'd been talking about some of the questions I'm think-ing about to do with South Africa, our colonial history, the impact on our present moment, and so on. What he said to me was, "Just don't be too romantic." I asked him what he meant by that, and he thought a bit and said, "Well, it's not just that something's been lost. It's that something's been broken, smashed."

And that gave me pause. It made me notice in my own writing a pull toward being wistful about loss, nostalgic even. When actually what we need to be saying very clearly is that the particular time we're living in is one in which something precious has been broken, smashed. That some things are gone, not just lost.

LOPEZ: I think probably my approach is that much has been lost, but not irretrievably lost.

MARTIN: Yes.

LOPEZ: And yes, great damage has been done. We've lost languages and cultures and particular species of animals, and we've abandoned worthy projects. But we're not prisoners of time.

The possibility to evolve in an unprecedented direction is always before us. And one of the things that the components of landscape teach you is that everything does not grow at the same rate or change at the same rate. So the rate of change per unit of time for the boulders in the middle of the river is not the same as it is for these ash trees, and certainly not the same for those—

Here comes another one by itself, just flying up there.

MARTIN: Ah.

LOPEZ: Those two were together. No, they're both after her now. They've gone up there with her.

You know, the rate of change per unit of time for those mergansers is not the same as it is for those rocks. And when you see that, it tells you: things can change more quickly than you can adapt, and that components of the environment in which you live, and which would seem to be static and immobile, can change all of a sudden.

If you could—if you had the patience for it and the event occurred—if you stood out here on this deck tonight and observed how many rocks formed the bottom of the river here that you can see in the daylight, one of them is going to move and you'll hear it. And the perception of somebody just standing there is: this is timeless. Because the overall movement of the river is so complex and the river is so animated, it will just spring a rock loose, and it will tumble twenty or thirty feet and come to rest again for another forty years.

What the river is saying is, the change that you think is never going to come has been here and gone while you've been making that argument. So this urges us toward preparedness. And the best preparation for being prepared is to be alert. To pay attention.

Of course, nobody can pay attention twenty-four hours a day. I mean, you go to sleep, and, you know, we like to watch a ball game once in a while or something.

MARTIN: [*Laughs*]

LOPEZ: But it's good to have that as a daily habit. I try to make a journal entry every day. But I also like to make myself present in a place where I'm really paying attention every day, through something that I don't understand. And it's not an attempt to understand anything. It's an attempt to keep the conversation going with the nonhuman world that surrounds you here.

MARTIN: It's a contemplative practice, really.

LOPEZ: It is. It's sort of indirect or unintentional. I asked Merwin one time, "What's the difference in the frame of mind when you are writing poetry and you're writing essays?" And he said, "Oh, well, the essay, it's much more intentional." And I said, "Well, I would say that with an essay, compared to what I'm trying to do in a story." I don't have an *intention* in a story. And I don't have an intention or an end point in engaging with the world outside myself. It's more like . . . you know, your practice of yoga or something. It's to stay aware. To stay aware of the presence of the world and what it is that is surrounding you.

MARTIN: About contemplation and awareness, you've been writing about your Catholic roots. But that's fairly recent.

LOPEZ: Yeah, it is. A lot went on in my youth, and I don't think I had any interest in talking about it until now. It just didn't attract my imagination. But among the things that's attracted my imagination now is the way in which revelation—to use the word in a nonsectarian sense—is politicized by people in power. The underlying message of the New Testament and the Christian Bible was politicized by people who wanted to build a church. Elaine Pagels has written brilliantly about the elimination of gospels written by women, for example, from the New Testament. And that tells you that the original message, if you will, has become highly distorted.

In a sort of simplistic way, I could say that I was exposed to Roman Catholic ceremony and theology when I was a young man in a Jesuit prep school. Which is important because the Jesuits, you know, are famously intellectual and metaphorical. And the head of the Jesuit order is called in Roman Catholicism "the Black Pope" because he's at such odds, or could be, with the more rigid and literal interpretation that is part of Roman Catholicism as it's practiced at the parish level.

MARTIN: Black as opposed to white in the sense that the pope is dressed in white?

LOPEZ: Yeah. And to give you an example: in the orthodoxy of Catholicism, you go to confession in a confessional, and you are given penance, which consists almost always of a set of prayers that you say. Five "Our Fathers," five "Hail Marys," five "Glory Be's," or whatever it is. But when I was in Jesuit prep school, you could go to confession with a priest in the back of a *cab*. As happened to me one time— my sins were related really [*laughing*] to acts of . . . taking advantage of people by being a smart aleck, a smart-ass.

And my penance, the priest told me, was to go to the Metropolitan Museum, which was two blocks from the school, and find a certain painting and sit down in front of it and consider the relationships that were there in the painting.

MARTIN: That's extraordinary.

LOPEZ: I think that when I was young, I was exposed to Christianity as an *approach* to life, a way of organizing the spiritual dimensions of life. And I didn't have a violent parting. I just drifted away.

I became aware that much that I needed to know as a human being was not being taught at my high-powered university because it involved people who were not middle class, not white, and not male. For forty years after that I focused on trying to be present in groups of people who were very different from myself, whose epistemologies were different, and who did not have an end point orientation in the world, like going to heaven or something like that.

Now, after all this experience, I'm looking back over that education in my teenage years and thinking something very good was buried here. And I'm familiar with the rubric. So maybe I can go back and look at it. Dig out something from my own culture that is worth articulating again and saving. You know, a lot of traditional people will tell you: as a white person, we appreciate your interest in our culture, but what you need to do is to go back into your own culture and dig until you find the things that you abandoned or sold out on in order to create this landscape of power struggles and ownership.

MARTIN: Yes.

LOPEZ: Maybe that's what's going on. But, as I told you at lunch, I've not written very much about myself intentionally because, in my early years, I thought, nobody's really interested in what you have say. So, don't try to tell us about yourself. Tell us something about *us*.

And now at the age of sixty-five I can say, I've been given a lot, and I'm going to go look at some of these things that I think are worth examining for the sake of the community of which I am a part. It's not about me. So, revisiting parts of your life that you couldn't put to use until now.

MARTIN: You've also been writing a lot about love in the last while.

LOPEZ: More explicitly.

MARTIN: More explicitly now, yes. In the earlier work it's implicit. I mean, love is there in something like *Arctic Dreams*, but it's not so directly expressed.

LOPEZ: I don't know whether you could say that's a function of my age and knowing that, God willing, I have twenty years left, or something like that. Or whether it's a sense of urgency that I have because of the things I look at in the world.

There is a courtesy and a deference and an accommodation that is characteristic of a certain kind of politics, international politics, where you are almost squeamish about confrontation. But my take on this now is that there must be confrontation, and there must be some way to replace war with reconciliation. And the strategies for the enforcement of a way of being in the world by extremes—extremists in Islam or extremists in Christianity—delay us in trying to come up with a way to cooperate with each other. Everybody is going to have to get by with less. So the people that have a lot now should not be occupying as much space with their rhetoric as they are.

I'm curious about charity. A lot of Western charity is about self-congratulation. In fact, in *Resistance* there is a story about a young man who's caught up in his corporeal works of mercy, his charity in the world, and he realizes he's not being honest with himself. I think—

Oh, my gosh! There's a great blue heron hunting. She's going to really be difficult to see. Come over here where I am. Look right over my shoulder. Right over my head. She's looking right at us, turned her head sideways.

MARTIN: Yes, I can see.

LOPEZ: You see her?

MARTIN: Yes.

LOPEZ: [*Long silence, watching the heron*] I hike in the river sometimes.

MARTIN: Along the edge?

LOPEZ: No, in it.

MARTIN: In it?

LOPEZ: In it, yeah. Because it's slow going sometimes.

MARTIN: [*Laughs*]

LOPEZ: But way up there once, I lost my footing on the bottom and, oh, it was probably six feet of water. So there I was, moving much too fast to grab the bottom and then I just was—

MARTIN: Swept along?

LOPEZ: Yeah, swept along in the current. And having a bit of difficulty. I was tired from hiking. A great blue heron feather came by in the water, and I reached out and held on to it. It was my raft.

MARTIN: Ah.

LOPEZ: And eventually, a ways downriver, I got my footing. Anyway, distracted by the—

MARTIN: Beautifully distracted.

LOPEZ: It's a pattern of conversation I've noticed in traditional people. Even when they are in a house, the older men that I've talked to, they always take a seat right by the window. They're always watching out there. Conversation can be desultory because it's always interrupted for what's going on out there.

MARTIN: What's arising.

LOPEZ: Watching the weather. You know, watching, watching the wind [*bird sounds in background*].

MARTIN: What's that bird?

LOPEZ: See, it's still but it's not silent, now.

MARTIN: That's what you were talking about earlier.

LOPEZ: Yeah. And— [*birdsong again, long silence*] What is in front of me is what I was thinking about.

You know, I love this idea that . . . you want everybody to go to heaven and you don't want to go there till everybody can go. And I have that sense of service. It really deepened when I was in university. I never thought of myself as a writer when I was young. I loved to write, and I loved to see the effect that stories had on people, but I didn't think of myself as a writer because I kept thinking, "Well, you know, who cares what you have to say? [*laughing*] You're a nobody!" At the same time that I had that urge to write, to tell a story, I also had this urge to join the Peace Corps, to go somewhere and be of service. And those two things have always overlapped.

When I first began reading about the bodhisattva, I thought, *Oh well, this is a reification of the impulse, for me, of the storyteller and the helper, the person who wants you to rise up into a state of enlightened awareness in the world.* And that, I'm sure, does violence to a traditional Buddhist understanding of the bodhisattva. But, you know, I'm appropriating something that I think wells up in humanity—which is a desire to help—that many of us do not *do* very well with. Many people are not good parents. And many people in their work turn to chicanery, cheating, and violence, and cry themselves to sleep at night because they do things like that. I think you have to go a really long way before you find somebody who is irredeemably evil. I think many people are . . . lost.

And the world requires *profound* compassion. Profound compassion. And not judgment. I mean, compassion as opposed to judgment. To be compassionate and not to judge. Where are the touchstones for that?

If I could imagine a story—which I don't ever do—but, you know, if I thought, *Oh, I'd like to write a story about . . . an enlightened, compassionate person who did something good in the world*, that's kind of [*laughing*], it's like a coloring book story.

MARTIN: [*Laughs*]

LOPEZ: But nevertheless, it's what drives my sense of . . . Well, you'll get this in that story I gave you, "The Museum of Game Balls." Every once in a while I think I want to write about something that is a little bit *beyond* me. In the sense of something like the story "Light Action in the Caribbean." That's a very unusual story for me.

MARTIN: Yes, it is.

LOPEZ: And this one is too. But I think where this story comes from is from a sensation that I've had for some years now. The idea that we, say those on the political left, can just confront those on the right, and talk them into a more compassionate way in the world, is unbelievably naïve. And in this story, a character who thinks he's capable of exposing evil is in so far over his head, that . . . It almost happens after the story ends that he comes to the awareness he's just toying with something. Or he's being toyed with by something that he thinks he might be able to control.

So, ideas that I have about the condition of the world I'm sure come up in stories, though I don't write about them very directly. But when I finished that story, I thought, *You know, I'd like a while to just sit at the typewriter and write a set of stories that are like this.* Because it's new.

There's a huge distance between *Of Wolves and Men* and *Arctic Dreams.* And it's not just . . . You know, somebody, a dear friend of mine, said, "Oh yeah, you can really see the homework shining through in *Of Wolves and Men*" [*laughs*].

MARTIN: [*Laughs*] Well, you did do your homework for that, but?

LOPEZ: But the book that I'm working on now is as far from *Arctic Dreams* as *Arctic Dreams* was from *Wolves and Men.*

[*Looking out at the bank on the other side of the river*]
There is a road over there. There might be somebody on it.
I saw a flicker of a light. There's one person that lives there.
A bridge was closed, and so the only way for him to get to
his house is to cross over at another bridge and drive all the
way back on this old road that's in there. It's the only thing
over there man-made. You can tell that it's old-growth forest because of the variety of ages and the variety of greens
and the number of standing dead trees. The mix there is
not the monoculture you see around elsewhere.

MARTIN: Yes, I can see that.

LOPEZ: You are looking at some trees that are very old,
some that are very young. The species are all mixed. The
light-hungry ones are right down here on the water where
they can get a lot of light.

MARTIN: How old is very old?

LOPEZ: Here?

MARTIN: Yes.

LOPEZ: Four hundred?

MARTIN: Wow.

LOPEZ: Four hundred years, some of those guys. We'll look at
some trees tomorrow that are three, four hundred years
old. Now, you can see it right there, that ash tree is yearn-
ing to the light. Everything, all its energy, is up, out, into
the . . . into the corridor of light. This is the southern side,

so the presentation here is different here from the presentation of trees on the north side. Somebody just went by. It's hard to see in this light. Flying too high to be a kingfisher.

MARTIN: What kinds of animals come here, apart from birds? Who do you see?

LOPEZ: Around my house?

MARTIN: Yes.

LOPEZ: Black-tailed deer—oh, there they go, mergansers! Six of them.

MARTIN: Lovely!

LOPEZ: Black-tailed deer, elk, mountain lion, black bear, bobcat, raccoon, mink, beaver, several types of white-footed deer mice—

MARTIN: What are deer mice? Gary mentions them in *Practice of the Wild*.

LOPEZ: Deer mice? I think the genus is *Peromyscus*. They're just a small woodland mouse.

MARTIN: Okay.

LOPEZ: Voles, rabbits, a variety of snakes, thousands of different kinds of insects, coyotes, foxes. . . . And those would all be animals that I've seen right at the house. Or, you know, just looking out the window at the house. Except mountain lion. I've never seen mountain lion right at the house. But beaver live in the bank and in front of the house. And salmon spawn in front of the house. And, you know, my outbuildings have been torn up by bears and—

MARTIN: Do you see them?

LOPEZ: Yeah. In fact, when Emma [Hardesty] came here—she was Barbara Kingsolver's executive assistant—and Barbara moved from Tucson to Virginia.

MARTIN: Yes, she wrote about the move in that recent book.

LOPEZ: And Emma called me and said, "I'm not going to move with Barbara. I'm either going to retire, or I'm going to move to Oregon and work for you."

MARTIN: [*Laughs*]

LOPEZ: "Well," I said, "I don't know if I know how to have an assistant, and I don't know if I can afford an assistant." And she said, "Well, why don't I just come to Oregon and we'll see." So she came up here—they are really having a lot of fun now, those birds, up and down—anyway, she came up here and she met Debra and we went to dinner, and I talked to Barbara at length. And I decided, "Well, maybe it is time for me to have some help."

And the first day that she came to the house—and I'll show you where this is—the first day here, she walked down the path and there was a great big bear scat in the middle of the trail. And she said, "Oh, what's that?"

MARTIN: Bear-shit on the trail! [*laughing*]

LOPEZ: Yeah. So I said, "That's a bear." And I could see her thinking, "*What?*" [*laughs*] "Are they going to come while I'm here?" No, they're already here while you're here. They're watching. But they're not going to reveal themselves.

MARTIN: There was a mountain lion shot in Berkeley the other day in the parking lot.

LOPEZ: Wow!

MARTIN: I couldn't understand it. I thought, *Why didn't somebody dart the lion? Why did they just shoot it dead?*

LOPEZ: Yeah, that's the—

MARTIN: That's the way.

LOPEZ: Yeah, that is. Although the Mountain Lion Foundation in California would have darted it, if they had known about it. I'm sure I'll read about it in their next newsletter. You know, I love to use that word "lions," because it always throws people from Africa.

MARTIN: Isn't it great?

LOPEZ: Oh, come look at this one.

I turn off the recorder, and we go out to look at mergansers on the river.

CRAFT

Whenever Barry ventured out across the planet to do research for a story, his lifetime practice of seeing, feeling, and listening attentively to the patterns of the living world made him an intensely alert and curious observer. And when he returned home with his notes to write and rewrite and rewrite, it was with the same highly tuned sensitivity, awake to the precision of thought and the quality of the prose. On the second day of our conversation, we spoke about some of the practical work of making books and sentences: craft.

I asked if he had watchwords for writing that he might wish to pass on to others, and he began by mentioning respect and hard work, and some technical skills. Then he went on to talk about what he called hunger. "I cannot teach you hunger," he said. "And I cannot teach you discipline. And if you don't have those two things, the rest of it's just technique." When he was working in the field, he explained, the hunger to find out what he needed to know gave him a focus that was intense to the point of obsession, so that he'd set aside food and sleep and all the usual human needs and put himself "out there" in challenging situations, simply in order to discover what he was looking for.

Back in his writing room in the house in the deep forest above the home reach of the McKenzie River, he would write on a typewriter. Never a word processor. Unlike most of us now for whom writing is a text on the screen, something we track through, back and forth recursively, Barry would type a complete draft of a work, correct it by hand on paper, and then retype the whole text. Over and over again. Since our conversation, his account of it here has been instructive for my own work: just keep going bravely through a draft in the knowledge that you'll be coming back to revise. The description of what he was looking or listening for when writing and rewriting also made wonderful sense: the music of it, the rhythms of the prose, the precise patterns of sound and silence. But among everything I learned from him that afternoon about the craft of writing, it was what he said about vulnerability that I found most moving and also most encouraging.

For all his public status as a major writer, Barry says here that he would often experience a deep and private sense of doubt about his capacity to achieve whatever it was he was trying to do in a particular project. Over time, though, this characteristic experience of not-knowing became a kind of fuel for his work, even a weapon. It meant he was writing right at the edge of his capacity, and the insecurity of this helped to refine the text, make it better. Not everyone needs to work in this way, but for Barry, the agonizing sense that this time he really wouldn't pull it off became a familiar experience. And learning to recognize and reside with the pain of this condition became a necessary element in the writing process. As he put it: "And now at the age of sixty-five, I *know*, even though it's still very scary, that if I'm in over my head, that's where I'm supposed to be."

JM

JULIA MARTIN: What writers do you feel connected with at the moment?

BARRY LOPEZ: Do you mean in terms of correspondence, or reading their books, or personal friends, or . . . ?

MARTIN: Either/or.

LOPEZ: The people I seem to discuss *stuff* with—there are as many painters and photographers and dancers and composers as there are writers. Probably more. One reason for that, I think, is that when you speak with someone whose metaphor is different from yours, issues of career and jargon don't ever arise. You are forcing each other to get down to something deeper.

MARTIN: To what's really going on.

LOPEZ: I talk to Alan McGee quite a bit. The writers that I'm enthusiastic about now are younger writers whose work I think is really good and I want to find some way to promote it. And I go back and read writers from the nineteenth or early twentieth century, just to sort of check in to the history of which I'm a part. And I'm really interested in what drifts in to my desk from other countries, because it's a different take. I read books that come from people I trust. But—I think the case is the same for all writers—it's very eclectic.

MARTIN: Sure.

LOPEZ: I don't have a sense of what's "in." Or what you *should* be reading. Or what . . . what the *hot* thing is. I mean some of it's great and I do—by accident or something—stumble into it. But, you know, it's like the discussions I've had over the years with Cormac McCarthy. It's very infrequent that anything about writing is discussed. It's usually about . . . horses. Or about this world outside. And occasionally something political.

I don't talk craft, that I know of, with any other writers. I was very briefly at the University of Oregon to get an MFA in creative writing. But the program was just not anything that worked for me. And since then I've followed the same pattern, which is that I don't want to talk to anybody about what I'm writing. I want to write a draft and rewrite and rewrite and rewrite. And by the time I submit the piece, except for line editing, you know, it's pretty much done.

Debra is very different. Debra likes to share earlier drafts of work with other people she trusts. She's much more comfortable with being in a state of discussion about work with other writers than I would ever be. I just don't want anybody to see what I'm doing because . . .

MARTIN: Lifting the lid on the pot?

LOPEZ: I don't want to entertain somebody's idea about how to make it better.

MARTIN: Yes.

LOPEZ: When I'm writing, I'm already thinking about how it could be made better. And I never write from the middle or the end. I always start at the beginning and go all the way through to the end.

MARTIN: Just keep going.

LOPEZ: And then I start over and go through all the way to the end. And then I start—the same way I write a letter—I start over again and then go all the way through to the end. The first draft of *Arctic Dreams* took almost exactly twelve months.

MARTIN: Wow.

LOPEZ: And the second and the third and the fourth and the fifth. . . . The fifth draft took ten days. It's sort of getting down to the period of time in which a person might read the book. So I can sense when I'm going through on a second draft, "This is never going to hold up, but just keep going and then I'm going to come back."

MARTIN: Just get to the end and then start again.

LOPEZ: Yeah. Because if I saw what needed to be repaired, it would be so intimidating, you know. So I'm looking for a feeling of *"Okay"* at the end of each draft. And somewhere toward the end of the second draft, or maybe somewhere toward the end of the fifth draft, I'll know, *There's going to be a sixth draft with this.*

MARTIN: And you're not using a word processor at all. So it's a totally different thing from the kind of recursive looping that a word processor gives people the chance of doing. Looping through the same draft you're not doing.

LOPEZ: No, no, start all over. I produce something at the typewriter, correct it by hand, put it over here, and then create a draft at the typewriter that's sort of halfway between that and this.

MARTIN: Retyping the whole thing?

LOPEZ: Yeah, retyping the whole thing. But, you know the difficulty I'm having now is because so many people want an electronic version of the story. I do a first draft, take it out of the typewriter, hand-correct it, put it down, and write what I call a clean second draft. But the clean second draft is not verbatim this marked-up first draft. It's something that I'm rewriting as I go along. As I go along, I'm putting all this in but also rewriting right there, at the typewriter. So when I get to a third or a fourth draft, I give it to Julie [Polhemus], my current assistant. But then Julie enters a version of the manuscript that I have a *lot* of trouble relating to. And it's because her clean fourth draft is a kind of story that I never would have written.

MARTIN: But isn't she just typing out what you've put in?

LOPEZ: Typing exactly what's there. But she's not doing . . .

MARTIN: Oh, but you would do the extra layer.

LOPEZ: Yeah. She's not doing the layer that occurs that's never written down. So, I now have a difficult time toward the end, especially with the rhythms. There's a *music*, of course, in writing, and that music is very important to me because I think a lot of information is carried in the music.

MARTIN: Absolutely.

LOPEZ: At some point, I'm not going to be able to get my typewriters repaired, and then I'll have to learn this other way. And when I do then I'll figure out something. But I can't hear the story if I go back in and rework a paragraph. I've got to start all over again.

By the same token, if an editor says, "You know, something goes wrong in this essay right here." I'll think, *No, nothing goes wrong right there. But that's the place where you discovered that something was wrong.* So the problem is, maybe, in the paragraph above it. The disturbance occurred earlier, and the turbulence that it created is not noticed until . . . You know, it's like one of those rocks. The whitewater is *after.* So you're in the whitewater and you think, *Ha! There's a rapid here.* Yeah, but the cause of it is farther upstream [*laughing*].

MARTIN: I can identify with what you are saying about the rhythm and the music of the text, because when I'm writing something, I really need to hear it read aloud.

LOPEZ: Yeah.

MARTIN: I can't easily articulate what it is that I'm listening for, but I can recognize it if . . . if it's there. I find it quite difficult with students to try and communicate this, to try and teach them what to listen for, because I can recognize it, but I'm not quite sure what it is.

Do you think you could say what you feel you are listening for? Or perhaps that's too abstract. Maybe it's only in the particular sentence that you know what it is.

LOPEZ: It's all . . . it's all rhythms.

MARTIN: Yes.

LOPEZ: You can make what you are writing more comprehensible and memorable by attending to the rhythms of the sentences. You'll notice that something's wrong, something's not working. You are rewriting the same paragraph and doing it with your intellect, changing a word. But if you go back, you may notice that there was nothing wrong with the original language. The problem was that three sentences in a row were thirty-one syllables long. And it dulls.

MARTIN: Right.

LOPEZ: Borges. I heard him read once, in the early 1980s, at Columbia University in New York. Somebody in the audience said, "Is it harder to write poetry or fiction?" And without hesitation, he said, "It's harder to write fiction, because you must constantly change the *rhythm* of the prose in order to keep the reader engaged." So I thought, yes, I've never heard anybody say it, but I did agree in the moment with that.

MARTIN: And it's also in the pacing. You're wanting the reader to read a particular sentence more slowly or more quickly than another.

LOPEZ: Yeah. You can control what's going on in a paragraph in a number of ways. One, you can use a word at the beginning of a paragraph. I mean, it's not really conscious, I think, but you can go back later and discover what you've done by instinct or habit or something. You can say something, use a word in that first sentence, and choose a way to emphasize that word. It might be an adjective instead of a noun, and that adjective will *sink* like a rock through the whole paragraph, and you'll have it working for you all the way down. The reader will remember the connotation, and that connotation will expand through the whole paragraph.

Or you can end a paragraph with a five- or six-syllable sentence, and the last sound is a "d" or "t," something hard. Then you really don't need the period. It's there by convention. And by the same token, some diphthongs and vowels are so open that the paragraph keeps carrying. It doesn't really close off. So you can create a visual break, but the elision into the next paragraph just goes very smoothly. Whereas if you end it with a harsh consonant like that, then the next sentence begins much more on its own, independent of what's going on in the paragraph above. So, if there's a change of mood in the scene, that's something that helps establish a change of mood.

The funny thing—which I can say to you because you write—is that you're not doing that when you're writing [*laughing*]. You might be aware of some of these things as you come into a fifth or sixth draft. But you can go back and see . . .

MARTIN: See that it happened.

LOPEZ: See that it happened, yeah. And it's helpful if you're aware of those things. When you get stuck and you can't make a paragraph work, then you can think, *Oh, I wonder . . . I wonder about taking out this last sentence, which is an attempt to summarize.* And that will free the paragraph . . . of meaning.

MARTIN: Yes. I like that way of putting it.

LOPEZ: There's an interesting phenomenon in written language, and that is the control of meaning. It's appropriate in some places and inappropriate in others. I've told people when I've been in a workshop with them: when you use a locution like "There is," or when you see a locution "To this effect," or "which I will speak about in a moment," or if you see an exclamation point outside of dialogue, these are all signs that you are not doing your work as a writer. And they are the obvious places to go back in and repair.

I might work with some writers and say, "Go through the piece and circle the word 'it' all the way through, and then go back and look at it, and see if you can't find some alternative to 'It occurred to me.'" *What* occurred to you? It's okay to use that in colloquial discussion, but a reader— that's a different thing. And the specificity of what "it" is that occurred to you is going to get you a lot further with the reader than saying, "It occurred to me one day." You know, we are not engaged here with that language. That's not helping us.

So I think there are things that you can look at in your prose that help you *sharpen* the meaning, increase the clarity. But they're very subtle.

And if you do it for a long time, it's like blind rhyme in a poem, you know. The rhyme is not there on the page, but it's there in your head because the poet has set up the sequence and the meter to make that word that's not on the page explode in your head. And there's no reason why you can't do that in prose, though prose doesn't have the concision that poetry does.

MARTIN: People have often spoken about your writing as being very beautiful. Poetic, I suppose.

LOPEZ: Yeah, I know. But in the right set of circumstances, I always gently try to make clear that I'm not a poet. I have no ear for poetry.

MARTIN: Really?

LOPEZ: Mine is a narrative, not an imagistic sensibility. There are narrative poems, of course, that tell something like a story, but I don't have that gift for . . . a cascade of images that don't seem rationally to follow one upon the other but at the end seem perfectly linked and related to each other. I pay a lot of attention to language, and I think that's what people are saying.

I get into difficulties sometimes with copyeditors because they will tell me, "Well, you need to say 'the' here." And I'll say, "Well, no. It disrupts the rhythm of the sentence and it's not doing anything." *A* and *the*, the definite and indefinite articles, they have to *do* something or they shouldn't be on the page. And merely to put them in because that's the way it's always done just makes it turgid. The fact that it's not there is one of those things that keeps the reader alert. And if it really needs to be there I can guarantee you the reader will read it even though it's not there on the page.

MARTIN: Right. I'm sure you'd agree, though, that making beautiful things, beautiful words, whether you call them poetic or not, is obviously very important for you.

LOPEZ: Oh, yeah.

MARTIN: We spoke right at the beginning about a practice of awareness, and this seems to be part of the manifestation of that practice. To make beautiful things that are—

LOPEZ: Yeah.

MARTIN: —stories.

LOPEZ: That's why I'm so attracted to people like Tom Joyce, the blacksmith, or Richard Roland, the potter, or my friends here who are woodworkers. There is something similar. The making of pots and the making of door handles. Piece by piece they are beautiful. But they are also useful.

In some way I have a really isolated literary sensibility, but what I always come back to is: if I'm going to sit down and work really hard on it, I want it to be useful. I want somebody to read it and have an elevated sense of self-worth or possibility when they've finished the story.

I don't need to know them, but I love to put my hand on a handle and open a door that's beautifully set in the frame. And I want to do the same thing with a story.

MARTIN: It makes me think of my husband, Michael, who's a jeweler.

LOPEZ: I know he is, yes.

MARTIN: And hand tools is his practice.

LOPEZ: Yeah.

MARTIN: I'm thinking of what you're saying about making something that is useful. A story is not useful in the same sense that the handle of a door is useful, and jewelry too might seem not to be. But what Michael says is that jewelry is not a luxury. It is a necessity. It's what humans have always done. Way down in the archaeological record, you can see that we did that. We adorned ourselves.

So, the usefulness of that craft, and the usefulness of storytelling: maybe they work in a similar way.

LOPEZ: I couldn't agree more with him. You know, to have that kind of perception as a jeweler . . . that would be a jeweler I would want to be with, and play with, and explore something with.

People can miss the aesthetic in the everyday thing. And they can mistake the presence of an aesthetic for the presence of something, when in fact there's nothing there. It's *only* an aesthetic. So you can read some things that are beautiful. But they're not attached to anything that is important to the reader. They're like an unattainable thing.

MARTIN: Sometimes there are exhibitions of so-called non-wearable jewelry, which always seems like a very bizarre idea because jewelry has to be something on the body. That's what—

LOPEZ: Yeah.

MARTIN: —it's for. And you're saying in a similar way that a story is something the reader needs to be able to engage with.

LOPEZ: It's tricky ground, you know. After *Arctic Dreams* came out, I was so overwhelmed by the interest in what I was doing that I said to myself: I'm not going to write anything anymore. I'm simply going to live here in the woods and work on these large-scale pieces.

For example, I took what you call a sleeper, I think, a railroad tie, and set it in the ground in the woods, drilled the end, put a piece of steel in it, and drilled a large whale vertebra and put it on that point. And I set it in a place where if you walked along it would be so present and involved. I mean you'd have to back up and it was just this . . . opening in the trees. You would see it. And then it was gone. And that's what I wanted to work on: apprehension, and contrast, and scale.

Scale has become a really big thing for me now.

MARTIN: What does that mean?

LOPEZ: Scale? Sort of the river within the river within the river within the river. You know, the landscape between the second and third dimension. Fractals. Fractal geometry and fractal reality. And change. Recognizing the scaling in landscape, so that when you watch the wind move, there is the wind within the wind within the wind that has a similar pattern. The patterns are all expansions of each other, which is partly the way music works. And so on, just things like that.

But I wanted then to just work in the woods and make large sculpture, and I just was worn out with the kinds of questions that people would ask me about being an "adventurer." I would always have to say, "But, you know, I went with the people who do this. I'm not capable of doing this. And left on my own I probably wouldn't. I want to be with people who do these things." You know, if I'm diving into the ice in Antarctica, I want to be with people, watching them do those things, and I want to do them myself so my body has that experience. But, off my own bat, I'm not going to go and do something like that.

MARTIN: You always seem to apprentice yourself to an adept of some kind in whatever terrain it is.

LOPEZ: Yeah. You know, the cover of the American edition of *About This Life* is a boy standing on a beach watching men pulling in a boat. And when I saw it I thought, *Oh, that's it exactly*. He's the boy. He's the naïf. And he's watching, and trying to understand, and wants to participate. But he's separate.

MARTIN: Yes. But he's open. He's aware.

LOPEZ: Many years ago when I was traveling with Inuit people, they were hunting narwhal, small whale. And, you know, everybody gets a name. Or . . . let's see, a referent, really, more than a name. It's not like being blessed with a name. You know, white guy getting a name from the aboriginal people.

MARTIN: [*Laughs*]

LOPEZ: It's just the shorthand reference to you. It's informing to other people about where you fit in. So what they called me was Naajavaarsuk, which means "Ivory Gull." A person might say, "Oh yeah, ivory gull is a completely white gull. And you're traveling with these people and you're the white person." But that wasn't what it was.

If they were hunting walrus, and you bring the walrus out on an ice floe and open it up, there's a big gut pile. And when you're finished you leave the gut pile on the ice. And gulls come in, ivory gulls and glaucous gulls and black-backed gulls. All these gulls come in, and the larger gulls just muscle each other out of the way and come on the gut pile and tear it apart. And the ivory gull stands at the periphery and watches the whole thing. Then, while these gulls are pushing each other around, the ivory gull comes in, takes a little piece and backs out. And that's how they characterized the way that I traveled with them and participated. I was always slipping back out of the scene—

MARTIN: To write your notes?

LOPEZ: —to observe the scene. Not writing. They wouldn't like that. But they could see me as somebody who was very interested in watching the scene and was not participating in the scene all the time. So, kind of a strange thing, and the way they shorthanded it was to refer to this person as some ivory gull. That's what this person is like [*laughing*]. But it is like that. Boy's standing there on the beach. That's Naajavaarsuk, the ivory gull.

MARTIN: Learning from wherever you can.

LOPEZ: Yeah.

MARTIN: And then finding a space of quiet to absorb it.

LOPEZ: And really hungry. Carnivore. Never, never sitting still. Always getting into stuff.

On the same trip I was butchering a whale with a friend of mine. And—this is the edge of the ice floe, so two thousand feet of water right there—we had this narwhal out on the ice, and my friend was here and I was here. The whale's on its side. I opened the thoracic cavity, the lungs and the heart: driving a knife in, between the ribs, coming up between the ribs like this to the spine, and then reaching down, breaking the rib away from the breastbone and breaking it up like that, to open the cavity up like that, rib by rib.

And when I had gotten down this far—it's very slippery, a lot of oil from the whale, and ice, and it would be really bad to fall in the water there with your hip boots on, really cold water, so you're sort of trying to hold on to the whale to keep from slipping away—I got to where the diaphragm is. That's the end of the thoracic cavity. I made my cut up to the spine and then took the knife and just stuck it in the flesh above the abdominal cavity, where my friend could see that his work was starting now. Then I went back and took the end of the rib and brought it up like that and broke it away.

And he took the knife like this and picked it up to start his cut. And as he did, he looked away like that at somebody who was doing something but still carried through. And he drove the knife right through my wrist.

And, you know, we were thirty miles out on the sea ice and . . . it was an unfortunate thing to happen [*laughing*].

MARTIN: Wow.

LOPEZ: He felt terrible.

MARTIN: And you were bleeding everywhere.

LOPEZ: So, we boiled water and cleaned it and butterflied it, but I really couldn't use this hand very well for a while. And there was a door there for these guys, Inuit guys. Just kind of a racial thing, and they made sure they created a lot of situations where I couldn't do something because I didn't have that right hand. You know, they would always go to my right hand instead of my left hand. It's just a way of saying, "You're just a boy. With men."

MARTIN: But it wasn't your lack of attention that made it happen?

LOPEZ: It was just an opportunity to exercise an authority that they have. And to emphasize that I don't have that ability, however the accident happened. But during that same trip, you know I'd be participating in things, and then I'd go in my tent and zip the door shut and get my notebook out and write a bunch of stuff down. And then I'd come out.

My friend had said to me, "You know they don't want you to write anything down, and I think people know that you're in there, writing in your notebook. So, if you can just let it go until night, and we'll go back over the day." Of course there wasn't night, you know, it was July, twenty-four hours of sunlight at that latitude. After that our joke became that I wouldn't stop writing so he had to stab me [*laughing*] in my writing hand.

MARTIN: [*Laughs*] My goodness. Barry, you're telling me you're not this intrepid adventurer that people have imagined. But you have chosen to put yourself in pretty challenging situations, over and over again.

LOPEZ: I have. But you know, people have said, "Oh, it was very brave of you to write that," and I know that they're offering it as a compliment. But it isn't remotely connected to what I think of as . . . courageous. I guess that is what they meant, rather than brave. And by the same token, people would say, "Oh, you know, you do these things that are very dangerous." But I don't see them that way. I see them as what is *necessary* in order for me to discover something that I am so hungry to discover. And that's just the only way to do it.

MARTIN: Yes.

LOPEZ: There's a piece called "Southern Navigation," and it's about a trip in the Drake Passage between the tip of South America and Antarctica. I get seasick, and relatively easily. So I knew this trip would be one in which that kind of discomfort and inconvenience was going to be inevitable. But necessary. I'd made a Drake Passage crossing once before. I had to make that passage in order to get into the Weddell Sea in winter. So, nothing to be done. The second time I was in the Drake Passage I was on a German ecotourism vessel, and I was with my eldest daughter, Amanda.

MARTIN: Oh yes, I remember that piece.

LOPEZ: I recalled that a friend of mine had said about big water, it's like seeing the face of God. And that trip, I didn't get seasick. One of the great fears of my life has been being offshore in really big water, in pelagic waters. And in the Drake, you know, it's not that unusual to run into fifty- or sixty-foot seas. So there we were, and I was enthralled with it. That was a lesson in itself.

MARTIN: Why, do you think? Why did you not get seasick?

LOPEZ: I don't know. I think it had something to do with Amanda, and being responsible for Amanda. And wanting her to see icebergs and wanting to get her through her seasickness.

MARTIN: You couldn't be the boy then.

LOPEZ: Well, that was one of the things I had to consider. I had never been with a family member when working on a story. Part of what I was trying to find out was, "Can I do this? Can I be attentive to someone I love and at the same time be doing the same kind of *obsessive* work that I do?" When I'm working like that, I really have no patience with somebody who says, "You must eat now. You must sleep now." No. I must do *now* whatever it is that's calling me. And if I don't eat for a while, it doesn't even enter my head that I'm hungry. Or, you know, unless I'm falling down, I don't think about the fact that I'm tired and I've got to go do something like sleep.

MARTIN: Yes.

LOPEZ: But I mean it. To talk about it is to suggest that I'm some kind of fanatically devoted reporter or researcher. It's just about hunger. And it's not . . . Well, I don't know if it's unusual or not, but I'm getting credit for something that I shouldn't get credit for. Which is, in essence I'm not like other people. And the way I'm built, this is normal for me. The idea that I'm courageous or something just doesn't play into it. It's not *hard* for me to do. So to endure seasickness or other discomfort, that's really not entering into it at that point. I mean, it is terrible to be throwing up and headachy and all of that. But I'm so focused on what I'm trying to learn and how available it might be that I'm just doing the best I can.

MARTIN: So, with something like "Flight," you just put yourself through that kind of dreadful state of mind, flying days and days of nonstop flights around the world with planes carrying freight.

LOPEZ: I did, but I didn't realize until that moment in Cape Town that I'd broken through into something else. I talk in that essay about a photographer, Linda Connor.

MARTIN: Yes.

LOPEZ: And that it wasn't until I was completely time-drunk that I understood this place that Linda tries to photograph all over the world, which is . . . that time which is not owned by the oppressor. The landscape is owned by the oppressor, but the oppressor doesn't see, is not aware of, is not interested in time. And as long as people have that control of time which she photographs, they've got their heads above water.

MARTIN: Indigenous time, you called it.

LOPEZ: Yeah, indigenous time. You know, that story, "Flight," when I went to work with Northwest Airlines, the public relations man that I worked with said, "Well, we've set this up so you'll fly from home to Minneapolis, and then we'll put you on a flight and you'll go to Houston. And then you'll fly to Paris and you'll stay overnight, have a nice dinner. Then fly back to . . . I don't know, Los Angeles. And then fly here and then fly to Minneapolis." And I said, "Well, that would be a start. But what I need to do is fly a *lot*. I need to fly for days on end." And they don't understand things like that.

MARTIN: I suppose not.

LOPEZ: When I talked to the woman who was the public relations director for Boeing, and said I want to come up and watch the final assembly of a 747 400 freighter, she said, "Well, it happens at night." And I said, "Yes." And she said, "Well, you'll have to stay up all night." I said, "Well, no, I can do that." And she said, "But the cafeteria is not open." And I said, "Well, I can, you know, put things in a sort of lunch box. I'll be fine." And she said, "It just, you know, it takes hours and hours." And then she said, "I have a film that will show you final assembly on a 747 400. Takes about twenty-one minutes." And I said, "I can pretty much guarantee that there won't be anything in the film that's really useful to me as a writer. I have to *be there*. I have to touch it and smell it and hear it. And watch other people interact with it. And spend time doing nothing with it, in order to get it."

MARTIN: Like being by the river.

LOPEZ: Yeah.

MARTIN: Same . . .

LOPEZ: It is the same thing. But, you know, they don't understand that. I would say it's relatively common to go and talk to somebody who is explaining something to you about their professional life, and in twenty-four hours you'll know more about it than they do. Because the world that consumes what they produce is not interested in going deeper into anything.

MARTIN: And if you're used to going deep, then you can do it here or there or there.

LOPEZ: Anywhere! Anywhere. Yeah.

MARTIN: That goes back to what we said at the beginning about educating your grandson—or anyone—in awareness, or imagination, which they could take wherever they wanted.

LOPEZ: Exactly. Use it in any part of your life.

Anyway, I called her after I'd gone through final assembly, watching that. And I said, "I need to come back, and I need to go through the whole plane, with somebody who can explain everything in it to me." And it was just incomprehensible to her that somebody wanted this kind of information. She said, "I don't think there's anybody who knows that in our department."

And I said, "Well, find somebody who works on the assembly line whose job it is to run a checklist on the whole aircraft to make sure that everything's gotten done. And I'll talk to that person. And they can help me get through the plane." So she said, "Oh well, all right." And I came up to Everett and met this woman in her forties, very self-conscious. Hear that?

MARTIN: Yes, what was it?

LOPEZ: It sounded like a blue heron. Anyway, I met this woman. She was very self-conscious, what we might call a "working-class" person, and she said, "Well, I'm supposed to take you through the aircraft and show you and answer your questions." And I said, "Great. Let's start in the cockpit." So we started in the cockpit. And then we were in what's called the doghouse, which is below the cockpit, where all the avionics are and the nose wheel folds up in there.

MARTIN: You taking notes, or just remembering?

LOPEZ: Yeah, taking notes. So we've been doing this about three hours, and she said, "I've got to tell you, I was so scared to do this. I thought, *What am I going to talk to this man about? And why is this going to take very long?*" And I said, "Well, we've sort of just started and we're three hours into it. So that tells us two things: you know way more than you think you know, and I'm fascinated by everything you have had to say—I'm learning at every step. And we've got three-quarters of the plane still to go! So, do you want to break for lunch?" It was a great moment for both of us. She had a sense that, by God, she did know something. She wasn't making half of what those people in public relations were making, and they didn't know did-dly! [*laughter*] I said, "Much of the world, my dear, is like that. They're up there, polishing their résumés."

MARTIN: So there's the asking of questions again, the hunger, and being that boy. And just keeping on asking questions.

LOPEZ: Yeah. John McPhee says somewhere that you can't be afraid to look like a fool when you're doing work like this. You've got to be able to say, "I don't get it. Could you talk me through it again?"

And I tell people, if you know someone who is famous for having discovered something, ask them to explain it to you. And you'll discover a couple of things. One is, if they can't make it clear to you, and they're speaking in generalities, maybe they aren't as responsible for the insight as they would like you to believe. And if they do well with it, they will show you the outline of how you have to manage it, in order to communicate it to a reader.

But the temptation to become an equal with the person you are interviewing—it doesn't lead to a very interesting talk. You've got to be able to say: "I should read that, shouldn't I?" even if you have read it. And, "Could you go through it again? I'm still lost in this part." You've got to know if the person knows what they're talking about, or is famous for having said something that they can't understand.

You're there for the *reader*. You're not there to impress the person with your knowledge. Your knowledge doesn't count. You're a nobody. You're here for *us*. You're here for the reader. So, diffuse the situation and get every useful piece of information out of the interview that you can. If you do your work well, they'll see your piece and they'll say, "Oh, I didn't realize . . ."

There was a guy named George Hobson who ran the Polar Continental Shelf Project. It was kind of a thorn in my side. I needed his cooperation to move logistically all across the high Arctic, and he reluctantly helped me, and he needled me. A disgruntled kind of attitude. He always let me know that I was just kind of a nuisance in his operations. I had permission to be there and he had to follow through, but he didn't like it.

Now, when the book came out he wrote me this amazing letter, saying, "Why didn't you *tell* me what you were doing!" [*laughing*] I said, "George, I didn't really know what I was doing, you know? I was just trying to learn." So he said, "If you ever need any help, anywhere, doing anything up here, call me and I'll see that you get taken care of."

Another time, I wrote a piece for the *Washington Post*, and in it I quoted a man about his experience in Antarctica. He was the station manager, managing a research base. Some months later, I was in Washington at a meeting of Antarctic scientists. And he came up and shook hands with me and said, "We only met over the phone, but my name is Chip Kennedy, and you wrote about me in an article in the *Washington Post*." And I said, "Oh yeah, I remember talking to you." And he said, "Well, you did not misquote me. And you used my quotes in a way that made me sound much more informative and intelligent than I think I really am." And I said, "Well, given enough time, instead of just an interview over the phone, you probably would have put them together in the same way. They're your ideas. My job is to try to communicate them to other people." So he said, "Do you know about the *Nathaniel B.*

Palmer?" And I said, "Yeah, the big research vessel. The icebreaking research vessel." And he said, "Yeah, it's going to make a voyage to Antarctica in about eight months, and I think you should be onboard. I am the liaison between the National Science Foundation and the people building the ship. I'm going to have dinner tonight with the builders of the ship, and I'm going to recommend that they make space for you on that voyage." So, that's how I got onto it, that big, long trip, sixty-eight days.

MARTIN: [*Laughs*]

LOPEZ: It was because he felt that he had been shown respect for what he did. And as a result of that, he said, "I can recommend this person to go along." Thing is, you just can't get into situations like that without having somebody say, "I vouch for this person." I mean, all the work that I did after *Of Wolves and Men*. . . . I had made a few friends, and they just sort of passed me on to other people. And that's where *Arctic Dreams* came from. I didn't have to try to sell myself. I'd come into a village, and someone would say, "This guy is with me, he's okay."

MARTIN: What if you turn that attitude on yourself and say, okay, there's this boy, or this person, who has been talking to lots of teachers or adepts or skillful people from different fields and learning from them. But in the field of writing you are an adept as well. What would you want to pass on

to others about the craft from that perspective? I'm thinking of Italo Calvino, that lovely book he wrote at the end
of his life called *Six Memos for the Next Millennium*. It's
a sort of manifesto or a collection of watchwords, an exploration of the particular qualities that he's aiming for in his
own writing. For him, these include Lightness, Quickness,
Exactitude, Multiplicity. . . . But what would they be for
you? Do you have watchwords for your writing?

LOPEZ: Well, "respect" would be one of them. Respect the
people you are talking to, even if you don't like them,
don't share their politics. Respect the work that other people have done—the books, the magazine articles that are
the basic research elements of nonfiction. And respect the
reader. You show your respect for the reader by struggling
to create something that's welcoming and clear and engaging. And you respect the reader by doing your homework.
You don't get Richard Roland's birthplace wrong as I just
did. And you don't enter into an "I disagree with you" or
a challenging frame of mind with the material, until you
understand what it is that you're disagreeing with, and
then you *can* use confrontation to force a kind of clarity to
something. So, respect.

And then you've just got to be willing to work. I said
to somebody once, we can sit down for five weeks, and I
can teach you something about how to interview a person,

how to do research, how to tell bad research from good research. I can point you to people that will help you. We can look at paragraphs. We can look at the structure of the paragraph. We can talk about the arc of story. We can talk about the distemporal design of a story, so that a moment is here, it goes sideways like this, and then it goes back earlier and comes through that movement and ends out. We can talk about all that stuff. But I cannot teach you hunger. And I cannot teach you discipline. And if you don't have those two things, the rest of it's just technique. It's not going to go anywhere. So I would say that hunger and discipline are informing about this too.

Only a couple of times have I tried to explain what it is that I do to people with whom I was traveling. And in those times it never worked. It always went sour. It's much better if it's mostly about what that person does, and you're being an apprentice.

MARTIN: You're just doing it as it happens.

LOPEZ: Yeah. So insecurity, like naïveté, is a weapon, a way to—

MARTIN: Position yourself?

LOPEZ: Yeah, it's like your chi kung. The naïveté and that insecurity. I mean, you can look at my notebooks and see, "I have no idea what I'm doing." I write things like that to myself. "I'm in so far over my head . . ." And now at the age of sixty-five, I *know*, even though it's still very scary, that if I'm in over my head, that's where I'm supposed to be. And feeling lost and breaking down, actually breaking down in tears, because I'm feeling the depth of my own stupidity. Maybe it won't work this time. . . . But, you know, I've gotten through it before, and you just have to keep going, push through the fear.

When I'm with somebody, I'm tempted to say, in effect, "You know, I don't travel with people who require of me that I prove in some way that I'm worth their attention. I am here to listen, and I'm not interested in, and don't feel comfortable telling you anything, about who I am. If you want to find out who I am, go and look at a website or something."

MARTIN: That's not what we're doing.

LOPEZ: No. That's not what I'm doing. And if I have to prove myself, it irritates me. I'll do it. It's like getting seasick or something else. If that's what I've got to do to get what I'm after, I'll do it. But I don't like it. I don't like being treated as though, you know, the conversation is noblesse oblige, or that I should be very grateful that they are taking a few minutes of their time to talk to me. I want to be treated as a visitor from another discipline.

You've got to be uneducated to think that no one *knows*. This human enterprise, the part of it that is an effort to understand, is carried on by all cultures. And no one is in a position to tell another culture what to think—mostly because you don't know what they think. And on the outside, if they look like they are "primitives," maybe that means your point of view is not a very helpful point of view. You're not listening.

MARTIN: Yes.

LOPEZ: And all this has to do with what I think is a necessary frame of mind for the future. It's really time for those who've been talking a lot to listen. A lot of what I'm trying to do is to tell people, "Listen to others." Yeah, there's a lot of romantic *crap* about what indigenous people know, and they are perfectly capable of promulgating that view.

MARTIN: Absolutely.

LOPEZ: But there are elders in these cultures who really do know what they are talking about. The fact that these people are still on the face of the earth with a coherent culture tells you that they've consistently made the right decisions through drought and starvation and disease. They're still here. And they didn't get here by making wrong decisions. Somewhere along the way, a body of knowledge emerged that helps them survive. And we don't have signals out there in the world that we have created which tell us that . . . that we're surviving.

MARTIN: The opposite, in fact.

LOPEZ: Every time I get in an airplane, I look around and I think, *If commandos were on this airplane, we would be cooked meat.* I mean, if there were terrorists here. The idea that people get from television that they can fight evil, and the military can take over, and, you know, save them from the enemy . . . Walk down the aisles of a supermarket, and take a look at who you find walking around in a mall. There's nothing that tells you that in an emergency we are going to be able to do anything but panic.

That's a value judgment of mine, but I really worry that my people are not in the *least* prepared for what is coming. And they *will not* seek the counsel of other people. Because the color of their skin, or their gender, or God knows what, has made them think that they can't have the right answers because they're the wrong people.

It breaks my heart to think that everything that is developed, and what's culture, could be swept away because of this conviction that progress is a reality. Darwin was at pains to say that there was no progress, there was only change. And that it's not a teleological process. It's not headed for some divine end.

MARTIN: No.

LOPEZ: I read something the other day that really struck me about the discovery of life on other planets. The person writing said that if you ask scientists about the possibility of life on other planets, the physicists and the chemists, some of them will say, "Sure." But the biologists never do. Because they know, the odds against . . . well, not life, but humanity, human beings, beings like us. They know that—

MARTIN: The odds are so—

LOPEZ: Impossible. Complete accident that we're here. Marvelous interesting one, but complete accident. You need to sleep or make your notes or go to bed or something.

MARTIN: Why?

LOPEZ: It's late.

FLAMES

Barry was prescient, even visionary. He had no illusions about the apocalyptic seriousness of our global predicament, yet at the same time he felt a deep conviction about the sources of renewal in the patterns of the living world. After he fetched me from the airport, we had lunch and he said about *Horizon*, the massive book he was working on at the time, "I think what I'm doing is saying that the global situation is bad, it's a nightmare. . . . We don't see it yet, but it's worse than you imagine. It's like Cormac McCarthy's *The Road*." He paused and then continued, "But it's all right. In a spiritual sense, it's all right."

Still, our extended dialogue over the course of those glorious few autumn days took place in what feels in retrospect like a more innocent time. Before. It was before his cancer diagnosis. Before Trump. Before Covid. Ten years before his death. And it was before the great fire. In September 2020 the so-called Holiday Farm Fire consumed more than 173,000 acres of Oregon forest, including Barry's thirty-eight acres of deep trees, the ecosystem of the McKenzie River below the house, the old Toyota truck with its little bears, and the archive hut that housed the notebooks, typewriters, and other records of the writer's life he had built there over fifty years.

So, returning now to what he said to me in 2010 has been difficult. It has also felt necessary.

How may we as writers respond to a world on fire? The third day of our conversation beside the river began with this question. I reminded Barry of his anguish at the end of "The Naturalist," where he says, after a lyrical evocation of his home ecosystem, "To read the newspapers today, to merely answer the phone, is to know the world is in flames." I wanted to talk about how we put this dilemma of our condition together: the world is wondrously alive; the world is burning. His response, characteristically, was "Pick a place to live and become an apprentice." For Barry, that place was a river flowing through deep forest, and his fifty-year study was the complex syntax of its life. He says, however, that you might even do this in a city. The core practice is to become highly informed about the patterns of a specific place and then to "scale up out of them" into your work as a writer.

Following on from this, Barry goes on to ponder what it means for him for writing to be in this way a praxis, a way of life, even a prayer, in the midst of the present emergency. On the last day in particular, our dialogue seems to ramble and meander more than before. If he'd been able to edit the text himself, I feel sure he'd have wanted to pare it down and organize things into a clearer structure. But now with hindsight, the informality of it seems just right as a record of that morning's conversation: tracking the drift of thought wherever it leads, its freshness. We spoke about the relations between writing and the rest of one's life, about the negotiation between the ruthlessness of writing as an all-consuming focus and the need to respond to the demands of the everyday world, about neurosis and vulnerability and the sense of failure, about the need to be completely open when you travel somewhere to research a story, and about carbon footprint and the possibilities for innovation and transformation in the future.

When the great fire of 2020 came to the forest, just a few months before Barry's death, he and Debra and Mimsy the cat drove out in the middle of the night to make their way through high burning trees. When they were finally able to return to witness the devastation of their home, the deep forest was destroyed, his old truck was gone, and the entire archive of his writing life was burned to the ground. A few months later, Barry himself slipped away.

In years to come, as the forest and its inhabitants tentatively return, his place will be maintained by a trust, and the house itself, which the firefighters miraculously saved, will become a community space. People will be able to visit his beloved reach of the McKenzie River and to enter the private sanctuary of his writing room, which remains just as he left it on the day the fire came. But the deep hope in all this is for readers to visit Barry's writing itself, as we navigate the terrors of the fires to come. He wanted it to help.

A year now since his death, his voice comes back to me from the first morning of our conversation at a time when he was still well and fit, a keen reminder of that attitude of mind he so much wished to share. Once again, the catalyst for awareness is an apprehension of pattern. We were sitting under the old trees at the edge of the river, and he said, "I want to make a pattern in a story that allows a person to say, 'I remember what I forgot about what I meant my life to be. And I'm going to go do that now.'"

JM

JULIA MARTIN: Sitting by the river here, the world is so beautiful. And it's wonderful just to be in this place of deep forest and deep inhabitation by all sorts of beings. It brings to mind, of course, your essay "The Naturalist," a sense of simply being in one place, and an awareness that is built up over time. And that's some of what we've been talking about: developing a practice of attention and awareness, and how instructive that is, how instructive the river is.

But I was out here this morning early and I was thinking, *Okay, but toward the end of that essay you say something like*, "The world is in flames." The world is burning.

BARRY LOPEZ: Huh.

MARTIN: So how do we as writers put that together?

LOPEZ: Pick a place, I think. Pick a place to live and to become an apprentice. Doesn't really matter where. It can be in the city, even. I don't like the idea that there's something holy and better about living in a landscape like this, as opposed to living in the city. So pick a place in the sense of a geographical locale, and start to look for the patterns.

I think the only trouble you run into in urban areas is that there's an overload of patterns that are derivative in the sense that architecture is historically derivative. And then every once in a while something striking comes along, a reorganization of line and mass. When I was a kid in New York . . . Many parts of Manhattan are four square. The streets meet at ninety-degree angles, and the buildings, for the most part, are square to the corners. It's striking to see pigeons—who are reviled in cities as a nuisance—to see them fly, because the arc of their flight is always a contradiction of the local architecture. So when you're in an environment like a city, it's possible to slide backward without realizing it into a solipsistic set of references: everything is human, and everything must relate to a human intellectual architecture or an actual architecture.

So I think you pick a place where you have a reasonably good chance of recognizing the patterns around you, and then you scale up out of them into your work as a writer. This place here, of course, has relatively few patterns that were established by human social and economic organization, settlement if you will. For somebody like me who's spent a lot of time in museums, and a lot of time looking at paintings and photographs and sculpture, and has lots of friends who work in those areas, and who goes back and forth to New York or wherever, maybe in order to see people I work with, my memory is full of human pattern, human design. So what I want to feel when I'm here in part is, is there something missing? Is there something available in close attention here that can revise a troublesome idea? In the way human beings organize themselves to be governed, for example.

Traditional peoples, in my experience, have a syntax in their language that conforms interestingly, also weirdly, to local geography. And when you start to move out, or move deeper into who a people are, it's curious how much of who they are compares well with where they live. So if traditional people have survived all kinds of menace for tens of thousands of years, it seems like a good idea to probe that: the question of how we survive. Survivability, related to emotional, spiritual, and intellectual involvement in and awareness of local patterns.

When I say "pick a place," I would say, for some, become highly informed in one area. If you were wanting in a nonfiction way to rethink a dilemma, like global climate change, you'd need to have done a lot of homework, so that you do know what you're talking about.

There is also a kind of refutation for that second part of the thought that's available. And that is in the way corporations are organized with the chief executive officer at the helm. The CEO does not have intimate knowledge of all the working parts of the corporation. His job is to be able to appoint or recognize people in those areas that are really good at what they do, and invite them to have a conversation with him, and to take him very deep. And then he has to have the ability to surface and go to somebody else and go deep with them. And then surface. And in that process have a kind of overview of all the complexities and be able to perceive a relatively simple solution to a complex problem.

So those are two different approaches. I think writers can take that CEO approach too. Not picking an area where they want to have expertise, but taking advantage of going deep in different areas. Probably, if you lay out a continuum of fiction writers and nonfiction writers, it would be nonfiction writers who would focus on a single area in which they would have wished to become expert, and fiction writers who would be more interested in that kind of broad view. There's the specialized view and the broad view. And then, of course, people who do both would be where this explication just breaks down. It becomes ridiculous, you know?

MARTIN: I wonder about using the corporation as a metaphor. It feels rather uncomfortable.

LOPEZ: Well, I guess it should. The corporation exists to make a profit. And you don't write for profit. I mean, of course you do because you have to put food on the table, but the way I see story, the profit is incidental. A storyteller in a village would be of use in the village because she or he tells a story that's needed at that time. And conditions improve because of that story being told to those people at that time. And then later, somebody might bring a blanket or food or a goat and leave it at the entrance to the storyteller's place. So that's a courtesy and a part of the reciprocity that distinguishes relationships in small-scale human settlements historically. But the way it's devolved for us, or evolved if you prefer, is you write a story and give it to a magazine and the magazine gives you money. So you never see the faces of those who might want to listen to the story. And it's left to the publisher of the magazine to determine what the audience is for the story that you wrote.

MARTIN: Yes.

LOPEZ: Kind of odd.

MARTIN: Odd, yes it is, very. Potentially quite alienated. Thinking back to what you've been saying about picking a place and observing the patterns of a particular environment, my impression is that for you the pattern, or the syntax of things, is often more important than the specific meanings that are put into the structures of that syntax. How might that way of seeing things relate to the practice of writing?

LOPEZ: Well, for a writer, you're working with a wild animal, which is the language. And you try to control it with syntax and vocabulary. When I say vocabulary, I mean you're wrestling all the time with connotation and denotation in words. Early on, you understand what the denotation of words is all about, and you're able to use them in that way with some precision. But that really drifts toward a technical language. It's the long period of writing that trains you to the connotation of words. And what's really interesting about some people's writing is the facility with connotation. They're able to use an adjective in a way that makes you think, *Well, I never had thought of using that adjective in quite that way*. In other words, if there is a large range of connotation, or meaning, for a particular word, and some of it is used regularly but out there at the edges, it doesn't get used that often, a good writer—or a certain kind of writer—can take advantage of part of the aura of a word that's not often perceived because they are working so closely with the language.

MARTIN: Yes.

LOPEZ: So the relationship between meaning and pattern would be that meaning is something you simply cannot control. It's a wild landscape of the language that ultimately determines meaning. I can write a piece and you can read it, and I say, "Julia, this is what I intended." And you can say, "Well, I can see that. But I read this piece that you wrote in 1974 and it helps me understand that actually there is something else here that maybe you have forgotten."

What that means is that I have a general idea which I could go back and find in my journals in 1974, maybe, and I'm still thinking about it, and I've devised a pattern that I think will make it come to life in 2010. But the pattern is what I'm working with and I'm sort of in a . . . I'm in a constant state of ignorance about what the *meaning* of the piece is.

You know I told you the other day about this long essay of John Fowles's called *The Tree* that's been republished. The editor called me and said, "We're doing this book by John Fowles, and we wondered if you'd read the text and give us a comment for the back of the book." So I said, "I really am trying to do work now. I'm not doing anything like that. No, nothing personal about you and certainly not about John, whose work I think a great deal of. But I just don't have time to read that essay closely and write, you know, a couple of sentences. But I want you to know that I reviewed this book when it first came out in 1979, and I'll send you the review and if there's a line in there that looks good to you, feel free to use it." So he called me back and he said, "Well, we really think this review you wrote of the book could actually be the introduction to the book."

Now, the book that I reviewed then had a lot of photographs in it, and my review referred to those photographs, but the new book is just John's essay. So the editor said, "You know, the places in your review where you refer to the photographs—of course we would have to excise those. So why don't I send it back to you, if you're game, and you can, you know, just rewrite a little bit?" And I said—I was so proud of myself when I hung the phone up—"Why don't *you* edit it and send it to me, and if I like it then I'll say okay." You know, so I'm not—

MARTIN: Doing the work.

LOPEZ: Yeah, yeah. So he did a nice job of a little bit of editing. And I got the piece back and then of course went to work on it, and changed it quite a lot. So that's what I mean about a *pattern* of ideas that I set up in the review. It was okay for the time, but *so* much has happened so fast in the past thirty years that a piece that functions as an introduction has got to take advantage of the zeitgeist of this moment. Which was not the case in 1979.

MARTIN: Right.

LOPEZ: This sounds a little bit hazier, I guess, but I outlined once a story about a writer who wrote quite a penetrating piece when he was in his early twenties. And his whole life as a writer has then been writing that as a novel: to write that novel every couple of years, because things are changing so quickly. So he writes the same novel every couple of years, and that's his whole life as a writer, to rewrite the one book. And every time it's published it's fabulously successful.

MARTIN: [*Laughs*]

LOPEZ: And then the conversations about it have got to be: "Did you read . . ."—let's call the book *The Wanderer*—"Did you read *The Wanderer* from '79 or '83?" "Oh, I read '83." "Oh well, then it's very different. We're not talking about the same book."

And that whole existential bewilderment that people refer to all the time—you know, where do we go, and who are we, and what is the meaning of anything, etc.—is always part of the conversations about the book. Because the book can't be contained by an analysis. It exists in too many forms. It participates a little bit in the whole hydra-headed thing: how do you get a hold of something that will not be in one place at one time? Which is what modern mathematics and plasma physics and these other forays into meaning have been, the kind of stochastic environments that we're willing to live in, people didn't know about and weren't willing to live in earlier in the twentieth century. Before Einstein published his papers on relativity, before that, there could be a more black-and-white world. So Mendel, for example, wanted a new ABC of one plus one equals two. But quantum mechanics comes along and says, "There are many cases in which one plus one equals three." Oh, so welcome to the twentieth century.

MARTIN: In the stories you've written about people finding their way through modernity, with all its varieties of uncertainty, you seem to love characters who find clarity and focus in the practice of taking care.

LOPEZ: How?

MARTIN: Making the model ship, making the tapestry.

LOPEZ: Oh, yeah. "The Construction of the *Rachel*." "The Tapestry," yeah.

MARTIN: And the main characters in "The Mappist" and "The Orrery," all people whose attention is in the details. Often it's attention to a task that involves handwork.

LOPEZ: Yeah.

MARTIN: Or intellectual work, or both. Would you agree that's a key focus for you, the idea of care, with regard to your own practice, and in relation to the characters you're interested in? You spoke the other day about "respect" as a kind of watchword, but what about "care"? Obviously the word also has connotations of love and compassion, that kind of care.

LOPEZ: Sure.

MARTIN: But also in the sense of precision and attention.

LOPEZ: Ah, yeah. Well, I see it. I wouldn't have noticed it, I guess, unless you pointed it out. But that's again a perception on your part about something that is a consistency in the work. So you could say, well, this is a person who is apparently quite concerned about the relationship of . . . taking careful care of something. I mean, that man in "The Construction of the *Rachel*," he was trying to put himself back together.

MARTIN: Yes.

LOPEZ: And because he's been traumatized . . . You know, I'm now being an interpreter of my own story. I don't know if I'll do it very well. But I think he's been traumatized and knows that he needs a spiritual foundation again, and that's why he goes to that monastery. It's all there for him, but he's not fully into it. He's still repairing himself by putting part A into part B and tab C into slot D. That's what he's doing with the *Rachel*. But the monks around him, they get it completely. And so, you know . . .

MARTIN: Yes, it's lovely—

LOPEZ: —when things are ready to happen, they're packed and ready to go.

MARTIN: They're off.

LOPEZ: And he's the one who . . . He doesn't understand that by carefully attending to the practical matter at hand he will recover his spirituality. I think part of what's going on in that story is that the forty days and nights in the desert is not necessary for every person. For many people, the maintenance of family and getting food on the table, and the diapers changed, and the children to their lessons, and taking care of this kind of order, this also is a spiritual practice.

You know there is a Greek word, *praxis*, that refers to the behavior associated with maintaining a relationship with the divine. So someone would say, "What is your practice?" And you might say, "My practice is the practice of a monk according to the rule of St. Benedict," or something like that. Another way that word can be used is, "What is the nature of your prayer?" Meaning, not that you have a specified moment and a specified ceremonial context, or speak a string of words that have been memorialized in the religion of which you are a believer or an adherent, but that your prayer is your way of life.

For somebody like me, the idea that writing is a job or an occupation . . . that's not how I would see it. What I see is, I have a way of life. Writing is a way of life. Everything that I do, or think about, or participate in, is all turning over in my head as story. I don't see a lot of difference between who I am and what I do as a writer. It seems to be just that one is a continuation of the other, and I don't know where the line is.

MARTIN: It reminds me of Corlis in "The Mappist." He says something like, "The world is unfolding in the pitch-dark. We're lighting candles. And those maps are my candles." There's that sense of a practice that is both a light and a kind of votive, sacramental act.

LOPEZ: Right. And an important thing that Corlis says in that moment too is, "And I will not put them out or extinguish them for anyone." Meaning, the commitment to the practice is so profound, that . . . heresy doesn't enter into the picture. If somebody came to you and said, "You'd be a much more successful writer if you could somehow write some short stories about vampires"—

MARTIN: [*Laughs*]

LOPEZ: —then you would abandon what you were doing and write a book about vampires instead? I mean, *no*! But I've known writers who would. I remember a writer who was an acquaintance of mine many years ago, and he was doing all kinds of things. But he'd write a book about every three years, a novel of some sort, and he would always take his directions from his agent. His agent would call him up and say, "This is the thing that's really hot now." So, he'd take six months and turn out the hot thing and make a lot of money, and okay . . . But that's writing as a business.

It just occurs to me now that when I was younger, probably, some of my conversation with writers was truncated because the idea of social responsibility or the spiritual interior worlds, those were not ideas that traveled very far or were very often discussed, at least in public forums, writers' conferences, and things like that. And I used to feel . . . that I wish they were. And now I'm indifferent to it. My commitment lies in a place where I ask no one else to go, but I can't go anywhere else. It's kind of staggering to me sometimes that there is an audience reading that work.

Some books, *Arctic Dreams*, *Of Wolves and Men*, and that illustrated fable, *Crow and Weasel*, those have all been, in the conventional sense, best-sellers. Which is, you know, it's wonderful. But I don't think very often about how well something is going to do because that's not where my focus is. My focus is on how good can I make this. And how can I in the final stage find an editor who will work with me on the piece and not be distracted by what they want to do or by who they think I am.

When I was freelancing heavily in my thirties, and I would go to these remote places, I found that I was always better off with a woman editor than a man. One of the reasons was that men, some men, are very competitive. Their approach to the story was to say, "Well, I did this once myself." But women seemed to think, *Oh, that's so interesting*, and the focus was on how is the story going to work. And I was much more comfortable working with a person like that, saying, "Can I help you make this better? Because I know there are lapses here where the transition isn't quite right, or the word is . . . You know, there's infelicity here and there and the other place." I guess, now that I think about it, I've always had women editors with books.

MARTIN: You said the other day when we were talking about your putting yourself out there into dangerous, adventure-filled places, that for you it doesn't seem like a particularly brave act, though others might see it like that. But I think we ended that night with your saying that the act of writing does push you to the edge of what you can do in terms of what is scary. So even if the so-called adventures are not about courage, the commitment to writing may well be. And at the same time it's a practice, a prayer, a lighting of candles.

LOPEZ: Right.

MARTIN: And that means a real act of faith, of keeping going, persevering, in a context that is unknown and sometimes frightening.

LOPEZ: Yeah, I think you're right. One of the things that I've talked to other artists about—not writers, but particular kinds of people that are more like me—one of the things I would say is, "What do you think would have happened, to your work or to mine, if we were more ruthless?"

And what I mean by that is, we tend to be—or at least we tend to *think* of ourselves as being—polite, courteous, respectful of others, you know, all the good middle-class virtues. But a lot of successful artists with very powerful visions are so much in service to that vision that they don't care what happens around them. So their children are lost, their wives are lonely, etc., etc. And I've had that thought myself. I've thought, *What if I didn't care at all about anybody around me or my neighbors, or anything, and all I did was focus on the work?* So, instead of feeling a resentment that sometimes I can't control what else is required of me in an everyday world, if I just said, to whoever was involved in it, "Too bad for you. Fix it yourself, and I'm not going to be there." What would the work have been like?

Well, it would have been different.

And I do feel every day that I have not lived up to my own expectations. I feel every day the failure to . . . to create what I'm trying to create. I feel like I was given something and have been a miserable caretaker for whatever it is that I was given. That I lack courage. You know, when I say to a student, "I can teach you all these things, but I can't teach you hunger and I can't teach you discipline," I could say to myself at many points: "Insufficient hunger and insufficient discipline." That's what I think. That I haven't pushed as hard as . . . I was going to say as I should have, but who's to determine that?

MARTIN: Well . . .

LOPEZ: It's just an interesting question to take up with some friends, you know, when you're very vulnerable to each other. What would our lives have been like if we had just abjured all of the ordinary responsibilities of a human life? I think the answer is that we would have been on the verge of suicide for long periods of our lives because we would know that the degree of selfishness was unconscionable. I don't know how to . . . how to navigate there.

But I do know that I'm driven every day by the sense that . . . the life is insufficient. The attention to detail is insufficient. Constantly forgetting things, you know. I'd see a pattern here in the woods, and I'd think, *You know, I used to know about this but it's gone now*. I think that entropic reality is a very troubling thing for human beings. That no matter how integrated you *try* to remain every day, disintegration is the rule of everything. The entropic disassembly: here's the laminar flow of the water, and the rock comes in and it's disintegrated.

I think in neurosis the tendency is to photograph, or to . . . fixate on, the turbulence there and not carry through and realize that downriver, laminar flow occurs again.

MARTIN: Yes, indeed.

LOPEZ: And that every life has these kinds of disturbances, and you can't stop and say, "The laminar flow . . . I'm in a good place, and things are going to be fine." And then panic when you hit a rapid. When you hit a rapid, just move through the rapid and be assured that laminar flow will occur again. Coherence after incoherence. Coherence, incoherence. That is the reality.

The problem that people have, because being alive is so scary, is to become fixated either in the moment of beautiful sinusoidal laminar flow, which is Pollyannaish, or to become fixated in chaos, which is all the neuroses that are associated with self-destruction.

One more lesson from . . . the river.

MARTIN: From the outside, or for someone who is a reader, the kindness and compassion in your writing is really fundamental. And if you were imagining yourself as somebody who was taking that other track you describe, the ruthless track, it wouldn't be there.

LOPEZ: No, it wouldn't.

MARTIN: You wouldn't be doing the thing that you are doing.

LOPEZ: No, I see that. But did you read the story "The Museum of Game Balls" I just gave you?

MARTIN: Yes.

LOPEZ: Mr. Q is . . . ah, ruthless. And a formidable person. And this academic is an idiot. He just is so naïve about how the world works. He thinks he can come in and, through the force of personality and intellect, trap this guy into revealing what he was doing there in the Japanese occupation. Well, we fairly soon see that he's a boy on a man's errand. Nothing is going to happen, and he's lucky not to have been harmed. And who knows whose skin that was on the pelota when he's being driven back to the hotel.

MARTIN: Yes, it's very unsettling.

LOPEZ: I think that that story comes from a belief of mine that many well-meaning people who want to do battle with the world simply don't understand what they're up against. But my intrigue with Mr. Q is . . . part of my wondering: *can I understand a personality like this? Where there is no kindness, there is no generosity.* This is a person whose focal point, whose pivot point, is power and control.

MARTIN: He's got all the attention and precision—

LOPEZ: Yeah.

MARTIN: —without the compassion.

LOPEZ: Yeah, yeah, yeah. Exactly. With that kind of haircut for a man who is, you know, ninety years old—I can't remember exactly how old he is. He's very easy to see. He has those qualities of the snake or the rat. He's a menacing, lethal individual, and I wanted to make something like that because I don't want to have a frame of mind in which there's only one kind of person.

And when I finished that story I thought, *I wonder how far I could take this, if I could write a book like* Resistance, *that has a core to it, about people like Mr. Q and their triumphs.* You know all those characters in *Resistance*, whatever happens to them, we respect and sometimes revere them because they've made these decisions to do something. And whether or not they are successful is immaterial. But Mr. Q has made a decision to do something. And certainly Mr. Balewa is not going to be successful in controlling it or understanding it.

MARTIN: Right.

LOPEZ: But I've thought about this before. In *Crow and Weasel*, these two young men go farther north than anybody's ever gone. They have an adventure and return home. It's an archetypal story. But shortly after it was finished, I got the idea of wanting to turn it inside out and write another book about the Inuit people and their journey, encountering these two boys. So we would never know what happens to the boys, or where they come from. This story is told up to the point of encounter, and then it goes out into the Inuit world. So, I have thought of some of these stories, and about what would happen if you turned them inside out.

MARTIN: And also imagined pretty unappealing characters like Mr. Q.

LOPEZ: Well, part of what makes you interesting to yourself as a writer is your ability to get outside of your own thoughts. I think you can be naïve there and say, "Well, I've always worked . . . in marble. Now I'm going to work in . . . in granite."

MARTIN: It's still the same.

LOPEZ: Yeah. So for me, there's an essential tension. And what consistently gives me the thought that it's going along okay is if there is a newness. You know, like in "Madre de Dios," there's a structure that I've never known about before: pulling it all the way around to the end and then driving this thing backward through the whole story. That made me think, *Okay, I'm okay*. But I don't ever want to do the same thing again.

Then there's *Of Wolves and Men*. Whatever I was thinking about at the time, which I think was prejudice and the way in which we take the mysterious and try to control it, and define it, and the whole notion of our willingness to dismiss what educated people regard as unenlightened . . .

You know, if I had started that book with wolf children and werewolves, the book never would have gone anywhere. You have to have the biology and the ecology of the animal. And then another epistemology, and then introduce a moment like the genocidal chapters, before somebody reading about werewolves and shape-shifting, and wolf children and autism, says, "Oh, these things that I would have dismissed out of hand if they'd been prefaced in a different way are actually pretty interesting commentaries on . . . the maturation of our ideas about autism, and the awareness that we have as human beings that identity is sometimes terrifyingly obscure to us in another person."

We write stories all the time about a dimension of a person's personality that suddenly emerges and everybody is flabbergasted. "Oh, I never knew he was capable of this!" Well, that's what the werewolf story is about. You pick an animal that is the apotheosis of violence and savagery, and impose it on the parts of a person's personality that emerge in certain moments, when the moon is full or wherever it's going to be. That's how we think. But if the book were set up the other way, I guess it never would have worked.

If I think about a book of stories about people like Mr. Q, I guess it would be an effort to say, "Don't lose the sense of the continuum here. And don't be thinking that might is not right and right will out. There's no sign that that's going to happen."

You know, the dichotomy that is represented by Lucifer and Gabriel is a dichotomy that many peoples have memorialized in their folklore. In Christian folklore it's the banished angel and the angel that stays with God. And there is a reconciliation there. It's gray. It's neither the black nor the white. It's the gray. But when you're living in a world where people are frightened, they tend to divide in these fundamental ways. My way or no way. Black, white, Republican, gender . . . All of these things where people divide. But the middle ground is the one that you need.

MARTIN: The Middle Way, negotiating the binaries?

LOPEZ: And you can't have a proper social organization if you just have these two poles. It means no one is going anywhere.

MARTIN: Do you think that writing about people or situations that are quite horrifying in the way that Q is horrifying is part of your task in speaking to the present time, with its polar divisions?

LOPEZ: Yeah. And it's new work for me. It's something that is attractive to me because it's hard. I know that some people expect me to write a certain kind of thing, and that's because they've read very little of what I've written. I can't do anything about that. But I did learn early on that if somebody called and asked me to do something, and I took up that assignment, that sometimes it could go wrong. Because I wouldn't be doing what they expected. And I also saw that when somebody asks you to write a certain kind of story, they're already starting to work it out in their heads.

MARTIN: [*Laughs*]

LOPEZ: I don't want to be in that situation. In my life as a freelance writer, I banged on a lot of doors and wrote a lot of pieces and submitted them to a lot of people and things went along. And then people started calling or writing and saying, "We were wondering if you would do this." And you know in those moments I felt, in a conventional sense, "successful."

But it wasn't very long before I realized that that wasn't my way. I'd rather pay my own way, the airplane ticket or whatever it is, and write the story. And then go and say, "This is the story. And if you like it, great. If you don't, I'll go somewhere else." Trying to write *for* somebody who has expectations is like dealing with a sick animal in a closed environment. You never really get away from it, and the threat of being harmed is always there. I just don't want to confine it.

MARTIN: Ha. I'll remember that image.

LOPEZ: I think that that is fundamentally important in non-fiction. If I go to Sri Lanka and I have some ideas about the civil war, and what civil war is like in different parts of the world, and I get there and think, *Oh, my God, this is strangely different!,* then I can't be writing the story that I thought I might be writing when I arrived. You've got to be . . . completely open to what it is.

That's why it's always a good idea to find a few people to travel with. When I was traveling with some people that worked for Richard Leakey, in essence what they were saying is, "You've got a lot of reading behind you and you understand something about paleoanthropology, but you've never done this. And you're going to feel lost, but it's okay. Because we like you. We'll take care of you. But we think it's a good idea for you to get lost, because otherwise you're just going to write the story you came with. And why are we here, you know? For local color?" [*Laughs*]

MARTIN: [*Laughs*] Barry, how do you deal with the carbon footprint question? I mean, traveling is so basic to the kind of life you've lived over the last long time. But nowadays, we are so aware of the impact of jet travel. How do you put it all together? Or don't you?

LOPEZ: Well, the knee-jerk response is to say something like, "I'm trying to travel less," or something that sounds politically correct. You know, that god-awful concept.

I don't really think that much about it. Because for me it falls into the place where I think nothing's free and you have an obligation once you step on this plane. So when I leave here and I get on an airplane, a switch goes on. And from that moment everything is, by a measurable degree, more serious about responsibilities. When I arrive at a place and meet people, then another switch goes on. Which is, I'm in public now and I've got to be cognizant. And when I step on a stage, that's the highest form of it. You have asked for people's time. You had better be very good.

And when it's over, and I get to the room, lock that door. Then those switches go off, and I can let rush over me a tide of despair or hopelessness or anger or everything else that . . . It would be arrogant and irresponsible to show those emotions in certain public settings.

So the carbon footprint for me, the sense of guilt that I must have, is mitigated by my thought that, *You are now, we know, part of a group of people creating an intolerable carbon footprint. So you had better come home with something, some kind of enlightenment or some perception or reordering of pattern that helps us understand that this is not a good way.* It sounds like rationalization, but for me it's just part of what's going on at the moment.

You know, I recycle everything in my house. I mean, almost everything. I produce very little that I've got to take to the dump. But in another way, it's kind of a "so what?" Because I know the amount of material being recycled is so minuscule, and that capitalism works against recycling so strenuously that it's throwing the dishwater into the wind. But it doesn't stop me from doing it. It's what I call a technique of awareness.

You have these things that you do in your life that whether they're consequential or not is immaterial. It's the practice of minding when you are doing this that this orange peel must go into this place, and it will be decomposed by animals that live here, and eventually go back into the soil here. This piece of paper, you need to make the effort to put it in this box. And the box then goes into this big bag. And then it goes to this place where you dump it all in the bin, where it all gets chucked up and made into newspaper or whatever. The fact that it's an effort that really, to an accountant, doesn't make a difference, to me it does make a difference. It makes me aware that whatever it is that you are doing, you must do it in a way that helps. I have a lot of trouble flying if I'm going to do something that's just for me. But that doesn't come up very often because I'm never not . . . writing.

MARTIN: Talking about the capitalist machinery that we're all more or less implicated in, and how it works against recycling and sustainability, reminds me of what you said yesterday about Prometheus. We were up on the hill looking across at the Three Sisters, and you spoke about the myth of Prometheus, and how part of it tends to get forgotten.

LOPEZ: Well, the part of the Promethean story that we're most attracted to is the act of daring in which Prometheus stole fire from the gods. You can find that story probably in every human culture—the culture hero taking from the superiors a tool, an object, or a skill that improves the lives of the culture hero's family or village or culture.

But the rest of the Promethean legend that never seems to surface is that Zeus said to Prometheus, "In stealing fire—or the ability to create complex technologies—you have gotten something that's going to make life easier. But this is to some extent a delusion. It will be easier, but it will also be destructive. With the gift of technology, the ability to manipulate materials and make things from them, you've got to have two other things, and I'm going to give you those things. What I'm going to tell you is that without these two things, this technology that you've stolen, the fire that you've stolen will kill you."

The two things he gave Prometheus were justice and reverence. And justice and reverence, like courage, are among the cardinal virtues—that is, the characterization of behaviors in human beings all over the world that transcend religion. So, I wish that idea circulated more widely: that technological innovation that is not circumscribed by penetrating questions of justice and reverence is profitable but destructive.

I asked Oren Lyons one time why it was that Native Americans and other traditional peoples are invited to the table when the discussion is going to be about the imperiled environment, or spirituality, or these kinds of popular topics, but Native people are *not* asked to the table when it comes to questions of governance. Gut-wrenching issues about whether, for example, democracy is a useful form of governance in a time of extreme emergency. And Oren—he's an Onondaga chief—he said, "We're not asked to the table to talk about governance because for us, effective governance must include environmental awareness and . . ."

MARTIN: Spirituality?

LOPEZ: —and justice. Spirituality is what he said, but I think spirituality for Oren might include justice. So what he actually said was to point out that without spirituality and without environmental awareness, there can be no effective governance. And that's why we're not invited to the table because people who are talking about forms of governance don't want those issues on the table because they misconstrue spirituality as a plea for a certain kind of religious practice. And environmentalism is antithetical to the goals of capitalism.

We have a system of governance in the United States that is so compromised by capitalism and by the goals of profit—things or systems organized around the idea that to make a profit is the highest calling—that you're not going to have an effective form of governance. It's not going to work.

The great challenge I think in America is for America to reinvent itself. The reality of it arose in the minds of people like Thomas Jefferson, based on an interpretation of French philosophy and Enlightenment thinking. And it's never been achieved. The United States has come close. It's inventive and energetic, and has all the qualities that you admire in young people. But it doesn't have maturation. It doesn't have a sense of community before profit.

What it's doing is increasing the destructive. Look at American behavior in Iraq or in Afghanistan. Whatever the rationale is for the institution of the democratic principles of Enlightenment thinking in other countries, we're at a stage now, because of environmental tensions, where this kind of thinking is just not relevant anymore. So America is going to have to reinvent itself. Or it will go by the by, in the same way that England has. You know, its age of empire ended, and it has not known what to do since, except go along with the flow and act in public as though it was still the king and the queen running the show.

I think that if I see some rays of hope it's from these little flares that may amount to nothing all on their own, but they're lovely to see. In Bhutan, changing the idea of gross national product as a measure of the country's strength, or some other economic characterization for success in a nation, and looking instead at the gross national happiness index. You know it's easy to disparage and mock something like that. But the effort to say, "How does a state of spiritual poise—which is what happiness is—how does the incidence of that indicate the possibility for the future?" When you see things that come along like this, they are very encouraging.

Many years ago, in the eighties, maybe, I interviewed the minister of defense in New Zealand. New Zealand had recently announced, "You can't bring a nuclear arms ship into our harbors." And I said, "Historically, foreign policy is based on either military or economic strength. Well, New Zealand has no military strength and it has no economic strength. Wool's not that important!" [Laughter] "So, what are you leaning on here, to make this kind of statement? No nuclear weapons in our harbors." And he said, "Well, it's not military strength. It's not economic strength. It's our sense of dignity." And he went on to say, "The reason we have this awareness is because most of us who are in government here went to Vietnam." And that's where he left it. So what he was saying is, "Yes, in terms of conventional wisdom and the history of how governments work around the world, what we are doing is, you know, ludicrous. But we *are* doing it. And then, maybe another country will do something like that."

So when the Big Eight, or the Big Twelve, or all the economic powers get together to talk things over, they will realize that what they're talking about is not something that other nations are really interested in. And it doesn't serve them. And the idea that the elected heads of six or eight or ten governments are going to decide the fate of people in Niger or . . . pick a country. No. It's not going to work like that anymore.

MARTIN: Civil society. You see civil society and community as the crucial site of transformation?

LOPEZ: Yeah. I think the challenge—if I'm putting myself not as a writer but in an activist position—is, "Great. What's the apparatus?" I don't know. But in talking to people like Paul Hawken . . . Do you know Paul's work at all? He wrote a book called *Blessed Unrest*.

MARTIN: I know of it. About people's social and environmental justice organizations around the world.

LOPEZ: Yeah. Well, Paul is a genius. He's a force in so many ways. He understands how to clean up the economic mess that we're in. For example, he's now developing a silver fabric that comes in a roll. You just pull off a sheet and attach it, and you would have small-scale solar power in a little hut in the bush in Africa. And instead of the whole glass panel of materials, the heavy, economically successful manufacturing of these big panels for solar power, you just cut it off like a piece of fabric.

MARTIN: Wow.

LOPEZ: He is consistently able to come up with strategies that improve the quality of life for everybody and to write well about them. He's a charismatic person. At the end of "A Dark Light in the West," I make reference to him and to that book.

But anyway, when I talk to Paul about these things outside of something that I might write, what I want to say to him is, "What are we doing here? Where is the most promising invention? What does it look like? Of the many adumbrations, which is the one we should be focusing on?" You know, just play with each other. Not that you know where to go, but just stimulating each other to imagine, in a kind of free flow of ideas.

MARTIN: Yes.

LOPEZ: And those talks with people like Paul have been very helpful. When I go down to California next week, I'll meet a friend who's been filming in Papua New Guinea. He was there doing groundwork for the film at the same time I was in Australia, and I was seeing all of his stuff in Western Australia. He was dealing with the Chinese and tuna-processing plants in the north coast of Papua New

Guinea, and heavy metals poisoning in the rivers by Chinese mining operations and whatnot. The story had just broken about the successful Chinese bid on a massive copper deposit, and I recalled being in Tajikistan and watching a road being built and trying to figure out exactly what was going on there. Then I realized that it was the laying of a railroad to bring cheap, dirty coal from China to Afghanistan, through Tajikistan.

When I go down there on Wednesday, I'll have a meal with Toby and just trade ideas. "What did you see in Papua New Guinea?" You know, just have that sense of camaraderie and trading, that nobody's an expert here, but you just keep trying to put the stuff together. But I'm not doing it as a reporter. I have done reporting, and I have done journalism. But my place seems to be a bit different now.

MARTIN: Barry, is there any last thing you would want to say?

LOPEZ: No, I don't have that kind of frame of mind. I don't have a message to get out. You know, what I think of when we're together like this is, you're interested in these ideas personally, and professionally, and as a writer. And I'm glad to share them. I don't have a *goal*, really, or something that has to be understood about me. I don't think that much about myself, and I'm surprised when somebody says, "Well, who are you and what do you do?"

You must know all writers are ambivalent about whether or not they want to speak with somebody who wants to write about them. I think I've had a fairly good sense of who I wanted to work with and who was just not going to look deeply enough into what I was trying to do. They would be interested in the natural history or something, and that's all. But now some people are coming and saying, "We're interested now in all those years of work, what it is that's been going on here."

If there's some way to talk about what I do that's inspiring for younger people who are looking for what they want to do, that's . . . that's all I really care about. And you know I feel comfortable with you, so I'm not trying to project a thing that is ready-made. I'm trying to discover what it is that I do.

And when you leave, I'll throw all that away. Because I can't go and sit in front of that typewriter and think, *You're this, you're that, so you've got to do this.* I want to stay scared and off-balance every day of my life.

I switched off the digital recorder, and Barry went out to the deck of the cabin to look at the river. Then he called me to come and look at a cloud of hundreds of swallows swooping and calling to one another in the sky above the water. He said it was the first time he'd seen them do this. I said maybe they're gathering to leave for the South.

WORKS BY BARRY LOPEZ MENTIONED IN THE CONVERSATION

Of Wolves and Men. New York: Scribner, 1978.

"The Orrery." In *Winter Count.* New York: Avon Books, 1981. 37–50.

"The Tapestry." In *Winter Count.* New York: Avon Books, 1981. 65–76.

Arctic Dreams: Imagination and Desire in a Northern Landscape. New York: Scribner, 1986.

Crow and Weasel. Berkeley: North Point Press, 1990.

"The Runner." In *Field Notes: Stories.* New York: Alfred A. Knopf, 1994. 145–59.

"Flight." In *About This Life: Journeys on the Threshold of Memory.* New York: Vintage, 1998. 73–109.

"The Construction of the *Rachel*." In *Light Action in the Caribbean.* 2000. New York: Vintage, 2001. 109–25.

"Light Action in the Caribbean." In *Light Action in the Caribbean.* 2000. New York: Vintage, 2001. 126–45.

"The Mappist." In *Light Action in the Caribbean.* 2000. New York: Vintage, 2001. 146–62.

"The Naturalist." *Orion Magazine* 20, no. 4 (2001): 39–43.

"Southern Navigation." *Georgia Review* 57, no. 3 (2003): 547–62.

Resistance. New York: Knopf, 2004.

"The Museum of Game Balls." *Mānoa* 22, no. 2 (2010): 97–105.

"A Dark Light in the West: Racism and Reconciliation." *Georgia Review* 64, no. 3 (Fall 2010): 365–86.

"Six Thousand Lessons." *Prairie Schooner* 87, no. 3 (2013): 17–19.

Horizon. New York: Knopf, 2019.

ACKNOWLEDGMENTS

Thank you to Jane van der Riet for your meticulous transcription of the recordings in 2010 and for calling the dialogue a gift of peace. To Tom Payton at Trinity University Press for your immediate enthusiasm for the project, and to everyone else at the press whose attentive work has made it into a book. To Michael Cope for your unrelenting support and the countless conversations that helped make this conversation possible. To Debra Gwartney for your warmth and insight. And more than anything, thank you to Barry Lopez for the rare blessing of your friendship.

THE McKENZIE RIVER TRUST

Part of the proceeds from the sales of this book will go to the McKenzie River Trust for the care of Barry Lopez's house and lands, which are now the trust's to maintain. The nonprofit land trust was formed in 1989 to protect critical habitat and scenic lands in the McKenzie basin.

2018

BARRY LOPEZ (1945–2020) was the author of *Arctic Dreams: Imagination and Desire in a Northern Landscape*, winner of the National Book Award; *Of Wolves and Men*, a National Book Award finalist; and, most recently, *Horizon*, named a best book of the year by the *New York Times*, NPR, and the *Guardian*. He was also the author of four essay collections and several short-story collections and was a regular contributor to American and foreign journals. He received fellowships from the Guggenheim, Lannan, and National Science Foundations and was honored by a number of institutions for his literary, humanitarian, and environmental work. Until the fires of 2020, he lived in Finn Rock, Oregon, with his wife, Debra Gwartney.

JULIA MARTIN is a South African writer and a professor of English at the University of the Western Cape. In addition to academic work in ecocriticism, she writes creative nonfiction with a particular interest in metaphors of interconnectedness and the representation of place. She is the author of *A Millimetre of Dust: Visiting Ancestral Sites* and *The Blackridge House: A Memoir*, and she collaborated with Gary Snyder on *Nobody Home: Writing, Buddhism, and Living in Places*, a collection of three decades of their letters and interviews. She and her family live in Cape Town, South Africa.